Growing in CHRiST®

Early Childhood
Teacher Guide

CONCORDIA PUBLISHING HOUSE · SAINT LOUIS

God Protects His People in Egypt and the Exodus

OLD TESTAMENT 2

Copyright © 2007, 2008, 2015 Concordia Publishing House
3558 S. Jefferson Ave., St. Louis, MO 63118-3968
1-800-325-3040 • www.cph.org

Lessons 1–4 written by Christine Behnke in consultation with Lorraine Groth
Lessons 5–13 written by Jessemyn Pekari in consultation with Lorraine Groth

Edited by Lorraine Groth

Manufactured in the United States of America

Growing in Christ® is published by Concordia Publishing House. Your comments and suggestions concerning this material are appreciated. Email us at sundayschool@cph.org.

Contents

Introduction

For the New User

Early Childhood is a nonreader level for children in preschool and kindergarten. It includes a Teacher Guide, Teacher Tools (for teachers), and Student Pack (for the children).

Features of the Teacher Guide

- Easy-to-use, four-step weekly lesson plans
- A weekly Bible study on the first page of each lesson to help the teacher prepare
- Reproducible student Activity Pages in each lesson
- Age-appropriate ways to teach the Bible story and apply it to young lives
- Themed snack suggestions in each lesson
- Songs, wiggles-out rhymes, and ways to involve children in active learning
- Quarterly supply list at the back of the book
- Perforated pages to make team teaching or small-group/large-group teaching easier

Teacher Tools

This packet provides the following resources for effective teaching:

- **Posters** (teaching aids and Bible story posters)
- **Storytelling Figures** (four pages of story figures for telling the Bible stories)
- **Bible Story Background Tent** (two background scenes to use with the story figures)
- **Attendance chart**
- **CD** (recordings of hymns, songs, Bible Words, and Bible stories; melody-line scores for all music on the CD; Activity Pages, Resource Pages, and a list of student Bible Words in PDF format; and song lyrics in RTF format)

Student Pack

You will need one for each child. This packet includes the following materials:

- **Student Book** (Lesson Leaflets and Craft Pages and a list of the Bible Words at the back of the book to send home with the children)
- **Sticker Pages** (three pages with perforated sections for each lesson)
- **CD** (songs, hymns, catechism songs, and Bible memory words songs)

Additional Teaching Helps

Call 1-800-325-3040 for subscription and cost information to order the following helps:

- *Little Ones Sing Praise* songbook and *Sing & Wonder* songbook
- *Wiggle & Wonder: Bible Story Rhymes and Finger Plays*
- *Happy Times*, a magazine for young children
- **Puppets**—find an assortment online at cph.org; Jelly can be used interchangeably with Sprout
- **Restickable glue stick**—to allow for repeat use in attaching story figures to backgrounds (order online or at cph.org, or find in the office supply section of your local discount store)
- **Church Year Worship Kit**—a great resource for teaching children about the Church Year (includes a Leader Guide, an altar poster with paraments and more, prayer posters, and a CD)

Early Childhood Format

Young children need a safe environment with predictable routines and the same caring adults each week to feel secure. For this reason, we recommend letting them learn in their own space, separate from the rest of your program, where they can relax, play, and engage in age-appropriate activities.

You can still make choices in how you organize your Sunday School session and space. Choose the option that works best for your program, or tailor the material to work for your local situation.

Option 1

This format works well if you just have one group of children with one teacher (or a teacher and helper). It is a traditional self-contained classroom where the teacher does all the activities with the whole group of children. If this format suits you, begin with the Welcome Time learning activities and work through the lesson as it is written, adapting the materials to fit your time frame and children's needs.

Encourage parents to do the Activity Page with their child at the beginning of class before they go to their own Bible class or other activity. This helps children transition into the classroom more easily. It also gives parents a better understanding of what the lesson will be about so they can talk later with their child about what he or she learned.

Make copies of Activity Page Fun (available on the Teacher CD) before class so each parent or helper has one. Set these out with copies of the designated Activity Page and the other supplies they'll need. If your class session is under an hour, omit the Welcome Time activities and start with the opening worship or Bible story.

Option 2

If you have a large number of children in your early childhood program, try a large-group, small-group format. In this approach, children gather in their own classrooms or designated space to do the Welcome Time learning activities.

These learning activities serve two purposes: they help children transition into the classroom, and they activate prior knowledge, building interest and readiness for what children will learn in the lesson. Encourage parents to do the Activity Page with their child during this time before going to their own Bible study session.

When it is time to begin, all children in your early childhood program gather with their teachers in one location for the opening worship ("Gathering in God's Name"). Stay in this location to have a teacher tell the Bible story to the whole group, or have children go back to their own classrooms again for the Bible story ("God Speaks"), told by their classroom teacher.

The "We Live" life-application activities can be done in two ways. Teachers can do these activities in their classroom with their small group of children. Or you can set up each activity as a station. Children divide into small groups and rotate to these stations or sites. Then, all preschoolers through kindergartners come back together again for the closing.

Preparing the Lesson

Joseph and His Brothers

Genesis 37

Date of Use

Key Point

Joseph was hated by his brothers, who threatened him with death and sold him into slavery, but he was rescued by God. God's Son, Jesus, was also hated and was killed for our sin. He is our deliverer from sin, death, and the power of the devil.

Law/**Gospel**

Hatred ruins relationships and separates me from others and from God. **Jesus' death and resurrection restores my relationships with God and others.**

Context

Rachel died as her second son, Benjamin, was born. The twelve tribes of Israel are complete, but Jacob's favored wife is dead. Now Jacob's favor rests with Joseph, Rachel's firstborn. Jacob saw his father, Isaac, before he died and now lives in his father's land, the land of Canaan. The sons of Israel are shepherds.

Commentary

The account of Jacob begins and ends with Joseph (Genesis 37:2; 46:4). God always provides a deliverer for His people. In the lifetime of Jacob, Joseph was the deliverer. Moses records the Christlike characteristics of Joseph in Genesis, his first book. Joseph is never depicted as sinning in his vocation. He was not sinless, of course, for there would be only one Sinless One, Jesus Christ. Instead we see Joseph fulfilling his God-given vocations faithfully, trusting in God's mercy.

As a son, Joseph reports the misdeeds of his father's other sons. As a servant to Potiphar, Joseph becomes chief of all his master's possessions and remains chaste despite the advances of Potiphar's wife. In prison, he manages the jail with diligence, becoming a leader among inmates. As the right hand of Pharaoh, Joseph rules with wisdom and mercy. Finally, as a brother, Joseph forgives all that his brothers meant for evil because he saw the hand of God working for good. In each vocation—son, worker, and brother—Joseph trusted God to provide him with all that he needed to support his body and life, to defend him against all danger, and to guard and protect him from all evil (Small Catechism, First Article).

Joseph bore the cross of being his father's well-beloved son. He incurred the wrath of his other brothers. God revealed to Joseph the future, yet his brothers, his father, and his mother refused to believe him. They even rebuked him. But just as Mary pondered strange and wonderful things in her heart (Luke 2:19, 51), so Jacob kept the matter of these dreams in mind (Genesis 37:11).

Joseph's cross was magnified by his brothers' betrayal into death. They cast him into a pit, while dreaming up a story of vindication. When greed overcame their desire for blood, they sold him into slavery. Reuben's weakhearted attempts were too little and too late. He valued favor with his brothers more than the life of his father's son. Good intentions do not produce good works. What humans mean for evil, God uses for good.

To hear an in-depth discussion of this Bible account, visit cph.org/podcast and listen to our Seeds of Faith podcast each week.

Lesson 1

Joseph and His Brothers

Genesis 37

Connections

Bible Words
For those who love God all things work together for good. Romans 8:28

Faith Word
Jealous

Hymn
Praise God, from Whom All Blessings Flow (*LSB* 805; CD 3)

Catechism
Lord's Prayer: Seventh Petition

Take-Home Promise
God works all things for good for me.

1 Opening (15 minutes)

Welcome Time

What you do: Before class, set up two activity areas. In one, put out copies of Activity Page 1, crayons or markers, and decorating supplies such as glitter pens, rickrack, sequins, and colorful yarn or ribbon for the children to use in decorating Joseph's coat. Make copies of Activity Page Fun (below and on CD) for parents or classroom helpers. Adjust talk as necessary.

In the other activity area, set out wiggle eyes or buttons, play dough, clothespins, pipe cleaners, and other embellishments so the children can make animals. *Option:* Use a handheld device to record each child telling about his or her animal.

Play the CD from your Teacher Tools. As the children arrive, greet each one. Give them a sticker to put on the attendance chart.

Say Hi, [Aiden]. I'm glad you're here. I wonder . . . do you like to get presents? **What is one of your favorite gifts? Today, you'll hear about a special gift.**

Direct children to the tables where you have the activities. Encourage parents or caregivers to stay and do the welcome activity with their child.

Activity Page Fun Get a copy of Activity Page 1. Show it to your child.

Say **This boy got a new coat. Let's color it together.** Work with your child to color and decorate Joseph's coat. **Today, you will hear about a boy whose father gave him a special coat.** Point to the box.

Ask **What is a gift you would like to get?** Listen to your child's answer. **Can you draw that in the box?** As your child works, remind him or her to listen to the Bible story to find out what happened to the boy and his coat.

MATERIALS NEEDED

1 Opening	2 God Speaks	3 We Live	4 Closing
Teacher Tools Attendance chart CD	**Teacher Tools** Storytelling Figures 1-1 to 1-5 Background A	**Student Pack** Craft Page 1 Stickers	**Teacher Tools** CD
Student Pack Attendance sticker	**Student Pack** Lesson Leaflet 1 Stickers	**Other Supplies** CD or paper plates & beanbag Crackers & cans of cheese Paper Plus supplies (optional)	**Student Pack** Take-home materials
Other Supplies Activity Page 1 (TG) Decorating supplies Play dough Wiggle eyes, pipe cleaners & other embellishments Resource Page 1 (TG)	**Other Supplies** Sprout Story bag Crumpled drawing		

Active Learning Encourage the children to make play dough animals. Talk about the animals they made. Ask if they can make a sheep with curly wool.

Say **Tell me about the animal you made. In today's Bible story, you will hear about some brothers who took care of sheep.**

Use your classroom signal to let the children know it's time to clean up and gather for circle time. Sing a cleanup song (Resource Page 1).

Gathering in God's Name

What you do: Gather the children, and begin with this opening. To teach about the Church Year, use the materials in the Church Year Worship Kit (see the introduction for more information).

Sing "I Like to Be in Sunday School" (*LOSP*, p. 11; CD 14) or another opening song

Say **Today, we're going to learn about a boy named Joseph.**

Invite the children to say the Invocation and Amen with you. Tell them "Amen" is the special word they get to say at the end of prayers, hymns, and others parts of the church service.

Begin **In the name of the Father and of the Son and of the Holy Spirit. Amen.**

Offering Have a child bring the offering basket forward. Sing an offering song.

Pray **Thank You, God, for everything,* especially our Savior, Jesus.* Help us to listen and obey.* Bless our Sunday School today.* Amen.***

*Have children echo each phrase after the asterisk.

Celebrate Birthdays, Baptism birthdays, and special occasions

2 God Speaks (20 minutes)

Story Clue

What you do: Before class, make a simple, childlike drawing, and crumple it. Put it in your story bag, and have Sprout drag your bag to your circle time.

Say **Welcome, friends! Our special friend Sprout is here with us today too. Let's say hi to him!** Lead children in saying hi.

Sprout: *(Hanging head, speaking glumly)* Hi, teacher. Hi, friends.

Teacher: Hi, Sprout. You sound sad. Are you okay? And why do you have my story bag?

Sprout: *(Holding head up)* Yeah, I'm okay. *(Holding up bag)* I put my drawing in your bag, so Lily wouldn't see it. But you can, if you want.

Teacher: *(Taking out the crumpled drawing)* Why is it all crumpled?

Sprout: My cousin Lily and I were drawing. She is so good. She even won the coloring contest downtown! I wish I could draw and color like her. But I can't. Mine turned out yucky, so I crumpled it up and stuffed it in your bag.

Teacher: Hmm. It sounds like you are a little jealous of Lily.

Sprout: Jealous?

Teacher: Yes, jealous. It's when you want to have something another person has or do something the person does. You want it so much that you start feeling angry—like the way you felt when you crumpled your drawing because you couldn't draw as well as Lily.

Sprout: *(Hanging head again)* Yeah, I was pretty mad at Lily. I guess I'm jealous.

Teacher: I have an idea. Instead of being mad at Lily, why don't you ask her to show you how to draw better?

Sprout: That's a good idea! I'm going to go ask her right now! Bye, everyone.

Say **Girls and boys, Sprout isn't the only one to feel jealous of someone else. Talking to him reminded me of some brothers in the Bible who were so jealous of their brother that they did a very mean thing. I wonder what they did?** Accept a few suggestions. **Let's find out.**

Bible Story Time

What you do: Use Background A and the story figures to teach the Bible story. Use a restickable glue stick (see Introduction for more information), doublestick tape, or loops of tape to attach the figures to the background. Put the figures in your Bible, and remind the children that this is a true story from God's Word. To get children's attention, hold up your hand or a picture of Jesus.

Say **I need to see everyone's eyes here** (show hand or poster) **so I know you are ready to listen to our story from God's Word.** Open your Bible.

Say **God's Word tells us about a man named Jacob. Jacob had twelve sons. One of Jacob's sons was named Joseph.** Show Joseph (1-1), and add him to Background A. **Ten of Joseph's brothers were older than he was. One was younger. Jacob loved all his children, but he loved Joseph best.**

One day, Jacob gave Joseph a special gift. It was a beautiful new coat. Add coat (1-3). **This made Joseph's brothers angry.** Add brothers (1-2). **They were jealous of Joseph and said mean things about him.** Remove brothers and Joseph.

One night, Joseph had a dream. The next day, he told his brothers about it. He said, "In my dream, we were tying wheat into bundles. My bundle was standing up. Then, your bundles gathered around it and bowed down." Add wheat (1-4). **Now, the brothers were really angry at Joseph. They laughed at him and asked, "Do you think you are better than we are? Do you think you are our king?"** Remove 1-4.

The more the brothers thought about Joseph, the more jealous and angry they felt. One brother said, "He makes me so mad!" Another brother said, "I hate him!"

After that, Joseph's brothers took the sheep far from home to find some good grass to eat. One day, Jacob told Joseph, "Go, find your brothers and see if they are okay." So off Joseph went to look for his brothers.

The brothers saw Joseph coming. Add brothers (1-2); add Joseph (1-1) wearing his coat (1-3) on opposite side. **They said, "Here comes that dreamer, Joseph." Joseph's brothers were still angry and jealous. They planned to hurt Joseph.**

Then Reuben, the oldest brother (point to one of the men in the fore-front), **said, "Let's take his coat and put him in this deep hole." So, the brothers grabbed Joseph and took off his coat.** Remove coat (1-3). **Then they threw Joseph into a deep hole in the ground.** Remove Joseph (1-1).

Teacher Tip

Involve children in learning by having them put the pieces on the storyboard.

Key Point

God always provides a deliverer for His people and uses all things for our good. Jesus is our deliverer from sin, death, and the power of the devil.

All you could see was the top of his head. Poor Joseph!

After that, the brothers sat down to eat supper. Soon, they saw some men from a faraway country coming toward them. One of the brothers, Judah, had an idea. He said, "Let's not hurt Joseph. Let's make some money and sell Joseph to these men! They will take him far away; then, he won't bother us anymore."

So the brothers took Joseph out of the deep hole in the ground and sold him. Add well and brothers (1-5). **The men who bought Joseph took him to a faraway country called Egypt. Poor Joseph!** Remove all pieces.

When the brothers went back home, they lied to their father and said, "Joseph was killed by a wild animal. All we found was his coat." Add coat (1-3). **Joseph's father was sad. He cried and cried.**

Ask   I wonder . . . how do you think Joseph felt when all these bad things happened to him? Accept answers. **Was God still with Joseph?**

Say   Yes! God loved Joseph and was working things for good. God knew that many years later, Joseph would help lots and lots of people.

Ask   Have you ever been sad or afraid or alone? Accept answers.

Say   Sometimes, bad things happen to us too. But God promises in His Word and in our Baptism that He is with us. He loves us so much that He sent Jesus to be our Savior. He promises in the Bible (hold up Bible) to work all things for our good too.

Bible Story Review

What you do: Hand out Lesson Leaflet 1, stickers, and crayons. Review the story using the questions; then, give children stickers to put on the pictures in the sidebar. Encourage children to do the activities on the back with a grown-up at home. For an active review, provide a colorful shirt for a robe and act out the story.

Ask   What is happening in the picture? Joseph's father is giving him a new coat.

What will Joseph's brothers do to him? They threw him in a deep well and sold him to some men (traders). The men took Joseph to Egypt.

Will God take care of Joseph? Yes. God cares for us.

How does God take care of you? Accept answers.

Do   Act out the story together. Assign the parts of Joseph, Jacob, the brothers, some sheep, and the traders. Provide a colorful shirt for Joseph to wear as a coat. Designate an area for the well. Direct the action as the children reenact the story. At the end, sing this song to the tune of "Mary Had a Little Lamb."

Sing   Joseph was the favorite son, favorite son, favorite son.
Joseph was the favorite son. His dad loved Joseph best.
His brothers sold him to some men, to some men, to some men.
His brothers sold him to some men. Now, Joseph was a slave.
God the Lord gave Joseph strength, Joseph strength, Joseph strength.
God the Lord gave Joseph strength, for He loved him so.

Bible Words

What you do: Mark your Bible at Romans 8:28.

Say   The Bible is God's Word. Show Bible open to Romans 8. **Today, we heard about Joseph and the bad thing his brothers did to him. Joseph might have**

felt scared and alone. But Joseph wasn't alone.

Ask   Who was with Joseph when his brothers put him in a hole? Who was with Joseph when the men took him to Egypt?

Say   Yes, God! God was working all things for good. God is with us and takes care of us too. Because of sin, bad things still happen. But God promises to work all things for good for His children because of Jesus, who paid for our sins on the cross. Listen while I read that promise from God: "For those who love God all things work together for good." Now do what I do and say the words with me.

Say		
	For those	Point to children and self.
	who love God	Point up.
	all things	Hold arms out wide.
	work together	Clasp hands and move in circle.
	for good.	Twirl around in a circle.

 # 3 We Live (20 minutes)

Use these activities to help the children grow in their understanding of what the Bible story means for their lives. Choose the ones that work best with your class.

Growing through God's Word

What you do: Use a permanent marker to draw a happy face on one side and an angry face on the other side of an old CD, or use a beanbag and two paper plates, one with a happy face on it and the other with an angry face on it.

Say   **Joseph's brothers were angry with Joseph.** Show angry face on CD or plate. **They wanted a special coat like his. They wanted their dad to treat them special too. Even though Joseph's brothers did mean things to him, God loved Joseph. He was still with him. He had a plan to make things work out for good.** Show happy face on CD or plate.

Sometimes, we feel jealous and angry too. Show angry face. **We do bad things; we sin. But God loves us. He had a plan to make things work for our good. He sent His Son, Jesus, to be our Savior. He makes us His children in Baptism and forgives our sins. Even when troubles come to us, God promises to be with us and work things for good.**

Ask   **How does that make you feel?** Show happy face.

Flip the CD in the air. When it lands angry face up, have the children think of a time when they have been angry or jealous. Give help as needed. If it lands happy face up, have them tell how God is with them and cares for them.

If you use paper plates, put them on the floor, and give children a beanbag to throw at the paper plates. Depending on the plate the beanbag lands on, have the children describe an angry time or a way God is with them. Conclude by showing angry face again.

Say   **Joseph's brothers did mean things to him. We get angry and jealous too. We do mean things. We sin.** Add cross over angry face. **But Jesus died on the cross to take away our sins. God forgives us for Jesus' sake.** Show happy face. **That makes us joyful and happy!**

Preparing the Lesson

Joseph's Troubles

Genesis 39

Date of Use

Key Point

The Lord was with Joseph and, through him, saved Joseph's family and others. God promises to be with us in every situation, and through His Son, Jesus, a descendant of Joseph's brother Judah, God saves us from our sin.

Law/Gospel

I sin when I do not want to live out my vocation or forget that God is with me in my troubles; these sins, like all sin, condemn me to eternal death. **Nevertheless, God is with me in all my troubles and offers me and all who sin His steadfast love and mercy for the sake of His Son, Jesus.**

Context

Joseph's brothers get rid of the dreamer. The brothers cover up their evil with lies and blood, and Joseph's father refuses to be comforted. The sons of the Egyptian slave woman (Genesis 21:8–21; 39:1; Galatians 4:21–25) sell the favored son of their father into slavery. Against his will, Joseph becomes the leader of an Egyptian household. The Lord is with him.

Commentary

The theme of God's presence in all of Joseph's circumstances is central (Genesis 39:2, 3, 21, 23). The Lord is always working for the good of His own. Joseph serves Potiphar well. Joseph knows how to manage details and oversee things. "The LORD blessed the Egyptian's house for Joseph's sake" (Genesis 39:5)—every unbelieving one of them. God allows Joseph to suffer while allowing his evil brothers to get off free. He allows Potiphar and his indecent wife to prosper. All this God does for the purpose of preserving His people and working good for those who love Him.

Joseph knows and accepts his vocation. Potiphar's wife does not know her vocation. It is not Joseph's role to share intimacies with this woman. That is Potiphar's vocation. So Joseph says no to her ambush and invitations with a muscular "How then can I do this great wickedness and sin against God?" (Genesis 39:9). It is sin against God, against Potiphar, against her, and against Joseph's own body and calling. And so it is "wicked." That's the right word—God's word. Joseph rightly sees everything that this sin will touch, and he answers well. He still gets no reward for it.

In fact, Joseph receives another cross. His newest humiliation is to go down even further, into prison. The godly one suffers. The Lord is with him? Yes. God is doing something with Joseph in another vocation—this one in prison, with shackled feet and an iron collar around his neck (Psalm 105:17–22). All this looks forward to another vocation.

"The LORD was with Joseph," Genesis keeps repeating. He was with the slave Joseph, the seduced Joseph, and the shackled Joseph. Through it all, the Lord showed him steadfast love. Love—so the Lord could save His people at that time and bless the nations of the world through Jacob's other offspring. Love—so the Lord could show you Jesus, steadfast love incarnate. God did all that, with Joseph, for you.

To hear an in-depth discussion of this Bible account, visit cph.org/podcast and listen to our Seeds of Faith podcast each week.

Lesson 2
Joseph's Troubles
Genesis 39

Connections

Bible Words
GOD, the Lord, is my strength. Habakkuk 3:19 (CD 7)

Faith Word
Trust

Hymn
Praise God, from Whom All Blessings Flow (LSB 805; CD 3)

Catechism
Holy Baptism

Lord's Prayer:
Seventh Petition

Take-Home Promise
God is with me and gives me strength.

1 Opening (15 minutes)

Welcome Time

What you do: Before class, set up two activity areas. In one, put out copies of Activity Page 2 and crayons or markers. Make copies of Activity Page Fun (below and on CD) for parents or classroom helpers.

In the other activity area, set out play dough and heart and cross cookie cutters. Play the CD from your Teacher Tools. As the children arrive, greet each one. Give them a sticker to put on the attendance chart.

Say Hi, [Charlotte]. I'm glad you're here! I wonder . . . do you ever have troubles—things that make you feel bad? Today, you'll hear about Joseph and some troubles he had.

Direct children to the tables where you have the activities. Encourage parents or caregivers to stay and do the welcome activity with their child.

Activity Page Fun Get a copy of Activity Page 2. Show it to your child. Have your child look for the hidden hearts with crosses, and color them.

Say Here is Joseph. Point to Joseph in well.

Ask How do you think he feels? Accept answers.

Say There is something hiding in the picture that can remind Joseph of God's love. Can you find it? Point to a heart with a cross in it. **Joseph had troubles, things that made him feel bad. We do too. But the hearts and crosses remind us that God is with us. He loves us and gives us strength. Look for more hearts with crosses. How many can you find?**

MATERIALS NEEDED

1 Opening	2 God Speaks	3 We Live	4 Closing
Teacher Tools Attendance chart CD **Student Pack** Attendance sticker **Other Supplies** Activity Page 2 (TG) Play dough Cookie cutters Resource Page 1 (TG)	**Teacher Tools** CD Poster A **Student Pack** Lesson Leaflet 2 Stickers **Other Supplies** Sprout Crumpled artwork	**Student Pack** Craft Page 2 Stickers **Other Supplies** Sprout Apple slices Paper Plus supplies (optional)	**Teacher Tools** CD **Student Pack** Take-home materials

Active Learning Have the children name scary situations or times they have troubles. Use the play dough and cookie cutters to make a heart with a cross inside it. Talk about how God loves us and is with us in our troubles.

Use your classroom signal to let the children know it's time to clean up and gather for circle time. Sing a cleanup song (Resource Page 1).

Gathering in God's Name

What you do: Gather the children and begin with this opening. To teach about the Church Year, use the materials in the Church Year Worship Kit (see the introduction for more information).

Sing "I Like to Be in Sunday School" (*LOSP*, p. 11; CD 14) or another opening song

Say **Joseph had many troubles. We will hear about some of them today and how God was with him and gave him strength. Let's begin in God's name.**

Have the children say the Invocation and Amen with you. Tell them "Amen" is the special word they get to say at the end of prayers, hymns, and the like.

Begin **In the name of the Father and of the Son and of the Holy Spirit. Amen.**

Offering Have a child bring the offering basket forward. Sing an offering song.

Pray **Dear Jesus, we pray,* Bless our Sunday School today.***
Open our eyes and open our ears,* That of Your love we may hear.* Amen.*

*Have children echo each phrase after the asterisk.

Celebrate Birthdays, Baptism birthdays, and special occasions

2 God Speaks (20 minutes)

Story Clue

What you do: Bring out Sprout holding a crumpled piece of artwork.

Sprout: (*Crying*) Look what Lily did! She's so mean! She crumpled up the picture I painted for my grandma. Grandma is sick, and I wanted to cheer her up.

Teacher: Oh, Sprout. I'm sorry Lily did that. That must make you feel sad.

Sprout: It does. I didn't do anything to Lily! I was just putting the paints away like my mom told me. But that's not all. After Lily crumpled my paper, she shoved me and made me fall down. That really hurt! Then my mom thought we were fighting, so she sent *me* to the time-out chair instead of Lily!

Teacher: Oh, Sprout, it sounds like you had a really awful, horrible, bad day! You were trying to do a nice thing for your grandma and obey your mom, but you still had troubles! That reminds me a little of our Bible story for today about Joseph. He tries to be a good worker in Egypt, but he still has troubles too.

Sprout: Really? What happened to him?

Teacher: Well, lots of bad things happened to Joseph, but someone was with him the whole time and gave him strength. I wonder who that was.

Sprout: Really? I bet it was his mom. Or maybe it was his grandpa!

Teacher: No, those are good guesses, but it wasn't his mom or grandpa. Why don't you sit over here and listen to the Bible story with the boys and girls so you can find out who it was? (*Put Sprout nearby.*)

Bible Story Time

What you do: Use Poster A. Tell children that when they hear you say, "God was with Joseph; He loved Joseph and gave him strength," they should point to themselves and say, "And God is with me!" Practice this ahead of time. Mark your Bible at Genesis 39. To get children's attention, hold up your hand or a picture of Jesus.

Say I need to see everyone's eyes here (show hand or poster) **so I know you are ready to listen to our story from God's Word.** Open your Bible.

This is a true story about Joseph. Joseph's brothers were jealous and sold Joseph to some men who took Joseph to Egypt. Tramp, tramp, tramp went the feet of the camels. Walk in place. **Over the sand they went. Tramp, tramp, tramp.** Walk in place. **Over the river. Splash, splash, splash.** Walk in place. **All the way to Egypt!**

Ask **How do you think Joseph felt as he was taken away from his home and family to a faraway place?** Accept answers. **Do you think God was with Joseph on the way to Egypt?**

Say **Oh, yes! All this time, God was with Joseph. He loved Joseph and gave him strength.** Lead children in saying, "And God is with me!"

In Egypt, Joseph worked for the captain of the army. God helped Joseph obey the captain. Joseph worked hard in the morning. Circle arms and lean right. **He worked hard at noontime.** Circle arms straight up. **And he worked hard at night.** Circle arms and lean left.

The captain saw the good work Joseph did. He put Joseph in charge of everything he owned. Joseph was in charge of the house. Make roof overhead with arms. **Joseph was in charge of the wheat in his fields.** Raise arms and sway. **And Joseph was in charge of his cows.** Moo.

Ask **Was God still with Joseph when he served the captain of the army?**

Say **Oh yes! All this time, God was with Joseph. He loved Joseph and gave him strength.** Lead children in saying, "And God is with me!"

One day, the captain's wife wanted Joseph to do something bad. But Joseph said no. He said, "The captain is my master. He trusts me with everything in the house." Make roof overhead with arms. **"He trusts me with the wheat in his fields."** Raise arms and sway. **"And He trusts me with his cows."** Moo. **"I will not do something bad to the captain and sin against God." Day after day, the captain's wife tried to get Joseph to do something bad. Day after day, God gave Joseph strength to say no.**

Then, one day, the wife told her husband a lie about Joseph. She said, "Your servant, Joseph, has been very bad." Shake index finger. Point out the wife and captain on Poster A. **The captain believed his wife's lie. He put Joseph in jail.**

Ask **Was God still with Joseph when he was thrown in jail?**

Say **Oh yes! All this time, God was with Joseph. He loved Joseph and gave him strength.** Lead children in saying, "And God is with me!"

The person in charge of the jail saw that Joseph was a good worker. Joseph worked hard in the morning. Circle arms and lean right. **He worked hard at noontime.** Circle arms straight up. **And he worked hard at night.** Circle arms and lean left. **The person in charge of the jail put Joseph in charge of the other prisoners.**

Key Point

The Lord was with Joseph so that His people could be saved and so that Christ, a descendant of Joseph's brother, could be with us in every situation and could earn our salvation.

Ask Was God still with Joseph in jail?

Say Oh yes! All this time, God was with Joseph. He loved Joseph and gave him strength. Lead children in saying, "And God is with me!"

Through all of Joseph's troubles, God was with him. Sometimes, people hurt us or things happen to make us feel scared or sad or lonely too.

Ask Is God still with us when we have troubles?

Say Oh yes! All the time, God is with us. He loves us and gives us strength too. Let's say, "And God is with me" one more time. Do so.

Bible Story Review

What you do: Show Poster A, and use the questions to review the story. Then hand out Lesson Leaflet 2, stickers, and crayons. If the children have been sitting on the floor, have them take a seat at the table for the review.

Ask **What is the woman telling the man?** She is telling him a lie about Joseph.

What will the man do to Joseph? He put Joseph in jail.

Who is with Joseph, even when he has troubles? God

Who is with you when you have troubles? God

How does God help you? Accept answers.

Hand out the leaflets, and direct the children to the pictures in the side box. Read the directions, and do the rhyming activity together (boat—coat; fan—man; bug—jug or rug). Students will need help to see some of these. Give prompts. Do the activity on the back of the leaflet, or give the children time to stretch by doing this action rhyme together.

Say **God is with us through the day,**   Circle arms overhead.
When we sleep and when we play.   Put folded hands by head; jump.
He watches over all we do.   Shade eyes.
When troubles come, He's with us too.   Cross arms in hug.
He gives strength to me and you!   Make muscle arm.
Thank You, God! We trust in You!   Fold hands in prayer.

Bible Words

What you do: Read the verse from Habakkuk 3:19 in the Bible, or play it on track 7 of the CD.

Say **God gave Joseph strength to obey God's Word and do the right thing. Still, Joseph had lots of troubles. He was even put in jail. But God was with Joseph. He loved Joseph and gave him strength. No matter what happened, Joseph could say, "GOD, the Lord, is my strength."**

Have the children name situations where they have fears or troubles, and lead them in saying the Bible Words after each thing named. For instance,

Great Idea!

Say **When the thunder cracks,**

Children: "GOD, the Lord, is my strength."

When my parents leave me with a sitter,

Children: "GOD, the Lord, is my strength."

Continue with a few more examples. Then remind children that Jesus died for them so their sins would be forgiven. They can trust in Him and not be afraid.

Option: Have the children make muscle arms when they say the Bible Words each time, or play the verse on track 7 of the CD and add actions as you sing along. Use a tablet device to record the activity. Play it in class for the children to see. Then send it to parents to watch this week.

3 We Live (20 minutes)

Use these activities to help the children grow in their understanding of what the Bible story means for their lives. Choose the ones that work best with your class.

Growing through God's Word

What you do: Use Sprout or another puppet to reinforce the lesson truths.

Sprout: Teacher, I feel sorry for Joseph. He was trying to do the right thing, but he still got into trouble. He even got thrown in jail! I wonder how Joseph felt.

Teacher: What do you think, boys and girls? (*Accept comments.*) I think Joseph probably felt sad or scared at times. But who did we find out was with him?

Sprout: God!

Teacher: Yes, God was with Joseph. He loved Joseph and gave him strength. God helped Joseph be a good worker. God helped Joseph obey the captain of the army and say no to sin. God helped Joseph be a good worker in jail. Through all Joseph's troubles, God was there to work things out for good. And even though he didn't always understand, Joseph learned that He could trust in God, no matter what.

Sprout: Sometimes, I don't understand why things happen, either. Like when I tried to make a nice picture for my grandma and then Lily wrecked it and I got into trouble! That makes me feel sad. Is God with me when I have troubles like that?

Teacher: Oh yes, Sprout! God has made us His children in Baptism. We belong to Him. Troubles and bad things still happen to us. But God has taken care of the worst thing that could hurt us—our sin. He did this when He sent Jesus to die for us. Because God did this, we know we can trust Him to keep His promise in the Bible to be with us and take care of us even when we have troubles. He will give us strength. Someday, God will also take us to live with Him in heaven, where there will be no more troubles.

Sing "God's Always with Me" (*Sing & Wonder*, p. 9).

Craft Time

What you do: Hand out Craft Page 2, crayons, and the four Joseph stickers.

Let the children take the lead in retelling the Bible story from the scenes on side 1. Have them find the correct Joseph sticker to put in each box. Turn to side 2.

Say **Here are some pictures of children who have troubles.**

Talk about each picture, inviting the children to share some of their troubles too. Remind children that God promises to be with us always, even in scary situations. Point to last picture, and talk about how our biggest trouble is sin.

Say **During our church service, we tell God we are sorry for our sins. The**

Teacher Tip
Rather than getting louder to get a group's attention, whisper! Children will quiet down in order to hear you.

Joseph Feeds Egypt

Genesis 40–41

Date of Use

Key Point

God used Joseph to save His people, all Egypt, and other nations from famine. He sent His Son, Jesus, to save all humanity from sin, death, and the devil.

Law/**Gospel**

My sin causes suffering for me and for my neighbor, and I cannot take care of it. **In His love, God takes care of my needs, both physical and spiritual, forgiving all my sins for the sake of Jesus, who suffered, died, and rose again for me.**

Context

Joseph was thrown into an Egyptian prison after the false accusation of Potiphar's wife. Yet he gained favor in the sight of the prison keeper. God, through the authority of the prison keeper, placed all prisoners under Joseph's authority. The Lord was with Joseph, and whatever he did, the Lord made it prosper.

Commentary

Joseph is an example of patience under the cross. Joseph's exaltation to second in charge of Egypt does not come about without suffering and pain. Only after years of God's forming, planning, and pruning of the rough branches is Joseph finally formed. Just like Abraham, Isaac, and Jacob before him, Joseph trusted the Lord's promises despite every appearance, and he waited for the Lord's time rather than force his own (Psalm 37:5).

God was with Joseph and granted him such outstanding faith. Finally, God comes and liberates him in a wonderful manner, even though Joseph's feet were hurt with fetters and he was laid in irons. Yet, unbelieving Pharaoh raises Joseph out of prison (Psalm 105:18, 20).

God uses the dreamer to interpret the dreams of others. He who dreamed about sheaves of wheat, the sun, the moon, and the stars now discerns the dreams of the butler, the baker, and even of Pharaoh himself. God spoke in visions and dreams and sent Joseph to discern the will and Word of the Lord. God was saving His people Israel through Joseph's hand (Psalm 105:16–17).

God's plan for the salvation of His people required Egypt. No one is as discerning and wise as he to whom God gives the Holy Spirit.

So Pharaoh elevates Joseph to the command of a foreign land. God blesses Pharaoh and his unbelieving nation in order to bless believing Joseph and, through him, all of the children of Israel. The Word and promises of God are sure. The time is coming for Him to call His Son out of Egypt (Matthew 2:15).

To hear an in-depth discussion of this Bible account, visit cph.org/podcast and listen to our Seeds of Faith podcast each week.

Preparing the Lesson © 2007, 2015 Concordia Publishing House. Scripture: ESV®.

Lesson 3

Joseph Feeds Egypt

Genesis 40–41

Connections

Bible Words
Your Father knows what you need. Matthew 6:8

Faith Word
Provide

Hymn
Lord Jesus, Think on Me
(*LSB* 610; CD 1)

Catechism
Apostles' Creed: First Article

Liturgy
Confession of Faith

Take-Home Promise
God knows what I need and cares for me.

1 Opening (15 minutes)

Welcome Time

What you do: Before class, set up two activity areas. In one, put out copies of Activity Page 3A and crayons or markers. Make copies of Activity Page Fun (below and on CD) for parents or classroom helpers.

In the other activity area, set out play dough, plastic knives, and toy dishes or paper plates. *Option:* Provide gems or buttons to add as ingredients. Play the CD from your Teacher Tools. As the children arrive, greet each one. Give them a sticker to put on the attendance chart.

Say Hi, [Jackson]. It's good to see you today! I wonder . . . what did you have for breakfast this morning? Let child share. **Where did your [cereal] come from? Today, we're going to learn about a time in the Bible when there wasn't much food and how God cared for the people.**

Direct children to the tables where you have the activities. Encourage parents or caregivers to stay and do the welcome activity with their child.

Activity Page Fun Get a copy of Activity Page 3A. Show it to your child. Help your child write his or her name on the page.

Say There is a lot of food hiding in this picture. Can you find it? Circle everything you find; then, you can color the picture. Where does our food come from? Talk with your child about how God knows what we need and provides food for us through farmers and store workers and you.

MATERIALS NEEDED

1 Opening	2 God Speaks	3 We Live	4 Closing
Teacher Tools Attendance chart CD	**Student Pack** Lesson Leaflet 3	**Student Pack** Craft Page 3 Stickers	**Teacher Tools** CD
Student Pack Attendance sticker	**Other Supplies** Story bag Bottle of water, fruit & paper heart Activity Pages 3B & 3C (TG) Beanbag Sprout (optional) Ring, necklace & robe (optional)	**Other Supplies** Sprout Bread Heart & cross cookie cutters Cream cheese or jam Toaster Paper Plus supplies (optional)	**Student Pack** Take-home materials
Other Supplies Activity Page 3A (TG) Play dough & toy dishes Resource Page 1 (TG)			

Active Learning Encourage the children to take turns making play-dough food and sharing it with a friend. This activity allows them to practice using fine-motor muscles and learn about how God works through our sharing of what He gives to provide for one another.

Ask **What is one of your favorite foods? Use your play dough to make it or some other pretend food. What will you make?** Let children make food.

Say **Now pretend that you have food, but your friend is very hungry.** Have children pair up with a friend. **How will you share your play-dough food?**

Sometimes, it is easy to share things, especially when we have a lot. Sometimes, it is hard to share. Today, we will learn how one way God cares for us is through sharing.

Use your classroom signal to let the children know it's time to clean up and gather for circle time. Sing a cleanup song (Resource Page 1).

Gathering in God's Name

What you do: Having a routine can be very comforting for young children. Use this opening format each week so that children become familiar with it. To teach about the Church Year, use the materials in the Church Year Worship Kit (see the introduction for more information).

Sing "I Like to Be in Sunday School" (*LOSP*, p. 11; CD 14) or another opening song

Have the children say the Invocation and Amen with you. Tell them "Amen" is the special word they get to say at the end of prayers, hymns, and the like.

Begin **In the name of the Father and of the Son and of the Holy Spirit. Amen.**

Offering Have a child bring the offering basket forward. Sing an offering song.

Pray **Dear God,* thank You* for sending Jesus* to be our Savior.* Help us to listen* and learn* more about You today.* Amen.***

*Have children echo each phrase after you.

Celebrate Birthdays, Baptism birthdays, and special occasions

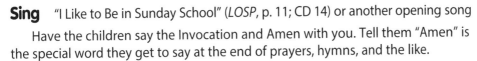

2 God Speaks (20 minutes)

Story Clue

What you do: Put a bottle of water, a piece of fruit, and a big paper heart inside your story bag. Use Sprout to introduce the clues and take the items out of the bag, or introduce the clues and show the items yourself without Sprout. *Option:* Instead of using a story bag, have Sprout show pictures of the items on your tablet device.

Say **Hi, friends! Our friend Sprout is here today too. Let's say hi to him.** Lead children in saying hi. Have Sprout respond. Notice he has the story bag.

Teacher: Sprout, I'm curious, why do you have my story bag?

Sprout: Well, I put some things inside it before I came because I want to play a guessing game with the boys and girls. I am going to give you clues, and I want the boys and girls to guess what it is that everybody needs. Okay?

Teacher: Okay, that sounds like fun. May I play too?

Sprout: Sure. Here's the first one. It is wet and cool, and you drink it. What is it? (*Let children offer guesses; then, have Sprout take the bottle of water from the bag.*)

Teacher: Water! You are right. That is something we all need.

Sprout: Here's the next one. You put it in your mouth, chew it, and swallow it. What is it? (*Let children guess; then, take out the fruit.*)

Teacher: Oh, an [apple]! Those are yummy! Food is something we all need.

Sprout: Okay, one more. You use your arms and gently squeeze. What is it? (*Let children guess; then, take out the paper heart.*)

Teacher: That was a tricky one, Sprout. A heart reminds me of love. Love is something we all definitely need too. Well, that was a fun game, Sprout. Thanks!

Sprout: You're welcome, Teacher. Well, I gotta go. Bye, girls and boys!

Teacher: Bye, Sprout! (*Children wave and say bye.*)

Say In our game, the clues were all about things we need. Today, we will hear about someone in the Bible who gave people just what they needed.

Bible Story Time

What you do: Copy Activity Pages 3B and 3C. Show the children where the story is written in the Bible so they know it is from God's Word. *Option:* Have a ring, necklace, and robe to put on at the appropriate time.

Say **Poor Joseph! He had so many troubles. He didn't do anything wrong.** Shake head no. **But someone told a lie about him, so he was put in jail.** Show Activity Page 3B. **Even in jail, Joseph worked hard. And God was with Joseph and blessed his work. God knew what Joseph needed and cared for him.**

One night, two men in the jail had bad dreams. In the morning, Joseph saw their sad faces and asked what was wrong. Make a sad face. **They told him they didn't know what their dreams meant and asked if he could help them.**

Joseph said, "Tell me your dreams, and God will help me tell you what they mean." God made Joseph wise so he could tell the men what their dreams meant. Make a smile face. **God knew what Joseph needed and cared for him.**

Many years later, the king had a bad dream one night. Lay head on hands. **In the morning, he was sad.** Make a sad face. **He did not understand what his dream meant. Someone told the king that Joseph could help him understand his bad dream. The king said, "Bring him to me."**

The king's men took Joseph from jail and brought him to the king. Joseph saw the king's sad face. Make sad face. **He asked, "Why are you sad?" The king told Joseph he had a bad dream and asked for his help.**

Joseph said, "Tell me your dream. God will help me tell you what it means."

The king said, "In the dream, there were seven fat cows (big moo). **The cows were eating grass by the river. Next came seven skinny cows** (weak moo). **Then all of a sudden—gulp** (gulp)**—the skinny cows ate the fat cows! Gulp! Gulp!"** Gulp, gulp.

God made Joseph wise and helped him understand the dream. This is

Key Point

God used Joseph to save His people from famine. He sent His Son, Jesus, to save all humanity from sin, death, and the devil.

Growing in CHRIST

what Joseph told the king, **"First, there will be seven years with lots of food for all the people.** Smile and eat food. **But after that, there will be seven years of no food to eat."** Hold tummy and look sad. **God helped Joseph understand the dreams. God knew what Joseph needed and cared for him.**

When the king heard what Joseph said, he was sad. Make a sad face. **He asked, "What will we do?"**

Joseph said, "Look for a wise man to be in charge of Egypt. During the seven years with lots of food, this man should take some and save it for the seven years with no food."

Now the king was smiling. Smile broadly. **The king said, "God has made you wise, Joseph. I want you to be in charge of Egypt." The king gave Joseph a special ring** (put on ring)**, a gold chain** (put on necklace)**, and beautiful clothes to wear** (put on robe)**.**

During the seven years with lots of food (pretend to eat)**, Joseph saved some of it in a special place called a storehouse. Then came the seven years of no food.** Hold tummy and look sad. **Joseph told his workers to open the storehouse and give the hungry people food.** Show Activity Page 3C. **Now, everyone had plenty of food to eat.** Pat tummy and smile.

God knew what Joseph and the people needed, and He cared for them. He made Joseph wise. He worked through Joseph to provide food for the people. God knows what we need and cares for us too. He provides food and the things we need to live. Best of all, God knew we needed a Savior. So, He sent Jesus to be punished on the cross for our sins. God forgives us for Jesus' sake and gives us a home in heaven.

Bible Story Review

What you do: Hand out Lesson Leaflet 3 and markers or crayons. Review the story with the following questions. Do the leaflet activities as you have time, or encourage children to do the activities with their grown-ups at home.

Ask   **What is Joseph telling the king?** He is telling the king about his dream.

   Who helps Joseph and the people with what they need? God

   How does God help you and give you what you need? Accept answers.

Do the sidebar activity on the leaflet together. Then, turn the page and have children put Xs on the fat cows. To get the wiggles out, sing the song on the back of the leaflet, inviting the children to name other things God gives us.

Bible Words

What you do: Open your Bible to Matthew 6:8, and read the verse: "Your Father knows what you need." Use a beanbag to help the children learn the words.

Say   **God, our heavenly Father, is our Super-Duper Caregiver. He knows what we need and cares for us. He provides all things for our good.**

Ask   **Can you name some of the things God gives you?** Accept answers.

Say   **Let's say our Bible Words together.** Have the children toss a beanbag to their neighbor on each word as they say the Bible Words. Repeat until everyone has had a turn to catch the beanbag.

Sing "God Cares All the Time" (*Sing & Wonder,* p. 17).

③ We Live (20 minutes)

Use these activities to help the children grow in their understanding of what the Bible story means for their lives. Choose the ones that work best with your class.

Growing through God's Word

What you do: Use Sprout.

Teacher: Hi, Sprout. Would you like to play the guessing game again?

Sprout: Sure, Teacher. But this time, you give the clues.

Teacher: Okay, I'll give you hints, and you guess what it is that everybody needs.

Sprout: I'm ready. Ready, girls and boys? (*Children answer.*)

Teacher: It is the people God gives us to take care of us.

Sprout: Oh, I know! Do you, boys and girls? (*Have Sprout encourage them to tell.*)

Teacher: Okay, let's do a harder one. It is something we all need from God when we do things wrong. What is it?

Sprout: Hmm. Girls and boys, do you know what it is? (*Accept answers.*)

Teacher: All good ideas. It's God's forgiveness.

Sprout: Do another one, Teacher.

Teacher: It is someone we all need who comes from God, and He was born at Christmas. What is it?

Sprout: I know this one. Girls and boys, do you know? (*Children suggest answers.*)

Teacher: Yes, the answer is Jesus, our Savior.

Sprout: Wow! God takes care of all our needs.

Teacher: That's right, Sprout. God gives us what we need to make our bodies grow. God gives us what we need to make our faith grow too. He makes us His children in Baptism and forgives our sins for Jesus' sake. He gives us His Holy Spirit. Through God's Word and Baptism, God the Holy Spirit helps us grow strong in our faith.

Sprout: Now, that's something to be very happy about. (*Teacher agrees.*)

Craft Time

What you do: Hand out Craft Page 3, stickers, tape, and crayons. *Option:* Cut out the figures of the king and Joseph before class.

Guide the children in recalling the dream the king had and what it meant for Egypt. Help children cut out the figures. They can add cow stickers and finish coloring the scene. Let them walk the figures like puppets in front of the scene. Point to the words, and read them for the children.

On side 2, have children add stickers of things God gives them. Again, point to the words, and read them for the children. To assemble the project, turn back to the front side. Help the children tape the figures to the *X*s; then, make the scene into a diorama, following the directions on the Craft Page.

As the children work, talk about the words "I believe in God, the Father Almighty" in the Apostles' Creed. Tell them that when we say those words, it means we believe that God made us and also takes care of us. He gives us what we need.

Paper Plus option: Copy Activity Page 3C for each child. Give the children seeds or rice to glue to the bag for grain. Have them draw pictures of their favorite food beside the grain sack, and color the page. Label it "God Knows What I Need and Cares for Me." Glue the page to a piece of colored construction paper to make a "frame." Punch holes in the top corners, and string with yarn to hang it.

Snack Time

What you do: Bring heart or cross cookie cutters, bread, a toaster, plastic knives, and a favorite topping (e.g., butter and jam or cream cheese). Avoid peanut butter.

Give the children a cookie cutter to make an impression in a piece of bread, or do this for them. Do not cut all the way through the bread! Toast the bread, and serve with butter and jam or cream cheese. The impression shows up. Talk about how God knows what we need and provides for us: food, family, Jesus, and the like.

Live It Out

Thank God for those who care for and share with you. To care for others, encourage children to bring a nonperishable food item to Sunday School next week to donate to your church's food pantry or to a local community food bank. As a reminder of God's care, have children draw crosses on the food containers.

Teacher Tip

Before serving any snacks, be sure to check with families for possible food allergies.

4 Closing (5 minutes)

Going Home

What you do: Gather the children's take-home things. Give children a chiffon scarf or colorful ribbon to wave as they sing. Have a beanbag for the activity.

Sing "Praise God, from Whom All Blessings Flow" (*LSB* 805; CD 3) or "God Is So Good" (*LOSP*, p. 57; CD 8)

Say **God knew what Joseph and the people needed and cared for them. He worked through Joseph to feed many hungry people. God knows what we need too. He will care for us.**

Let's say, "God knows what I need and cares for me" together. Do so.

Tell children you are going to play a game to think about ways God cares for us. Have them stand in a circle. Toss a beanbag to a child, saying, "God takes care of all our needs." Before the child tosses the ball back, he or she names something God provides.

Use some of the children's suggestions from the game in this closing prayer. Have the children repeat "You care for me" after you say each line.

Pray **Dear Father in heaven, You know what we need.**

When I need food, Children: You care for me.
When I need clothing, Children: You care for me.
When I need forgiveness, Children: You care for me.
When I need (*use ideas from children*)**,** Children: You care for me.
Thank You, God, for taking care of all our needs. Thank You for sending Jesus to be our Savior. Amen.

Reflection

Take a close look at your classroom. Is it neat and organized? Is it colorful? Are posters, chalkboards, and other items at a young child's eye level?

Find the hidden food in the picture.

Preparing the Lesson

Joseph Forgives

Genesis 42–45; 50:15–21

Date of Use

Key Point

Joseph revealed himself to his brothers and forgave them. Our Lord Jesus Christ reveals Himself to us and forgives us in His Holy Word and Sacraments.

Law/**Gospel**

The sin I refuse to confess troubles my conscience and separates me from others and from God. **In His mercy, God invites me to confess my sins and promises to forgive them for Jesus' sake.**

Context

Pharaoh made Joseph second only to himself as head over all of Egypt because Joseph was able to discern the dreams God gave him. The seven years of plenty were now over, and the seven years of prophesied famine had begun. The famine was so severe that Jacob's family, who lived in the land of Canaan, felt the effects of the famine and needed grain from Egypt to survive. Jacob sent his ten sons to Egypt for grain; only Benjamin, his beloved, did not go. The ten made the journey to Egypt, fully aware of their sin of selling their brother into slavery.

Commentary

Joseph recognized his brothers, but they did not recognize him. This provides him with an opportunity to bring his family down to Egypt. God used Joseph to save Egypt; now God is saving the family of promise by means of this heathen country. The promise given to Abraham, Isaac, and Jacob is the main focus of this narrative. God promises to give the land of Canaan to Israel. God promises to give Jacob descendants beyond measure. And most important, God promises that the Savior will be born within this family.

The ten brothers are sent to Egypt for grain. Jacob's decision to keep Benjamin at home to prevent him from "some calamity" is altogether human and foolish, as though Benjamin could not die at home, as though his welfare and life were in Jacob's power. If such a patriarch as Jacob, a man provided with great promises, displays such weakness, what courage can we have in dangers and trials?

These things are written to instruct and comfort us (Romans 15:4), in order that we may learn to trust God and work patiently in our God-given vocation. God gives us dangers, trials, and terrors so that we will learn to despair of our own strength and to rely on Him and His promises.

This was also the purpose of Joseph's meeting with his brothers. Joseph acted the way he did toward his brothers not because he wanted them to suffer for their sins, but because he wanted to stir up repentance in them. The terrors and troubles that this caused his brothers were not for Joseph's pleasure or revenge, but for the salvation of their souls. Recognition of sin must precede forgiveness.

Joseph reveals himself to his brothers at the great feast and forgives them, reminding us of how Jesus reveals Himself and forgives us in the divine feast of the Eucharist. Later, after their father dies, he assures them again of his forgiveness, telling them, "You meant evil against me, but God meant it for good, to bring it about that many people should be kept alive" (Genesis 50:20). In all, God's will is done. The brothers repent; Joseph forgives; Israel is saved from famine.

To hear an in-depth discussion of this Bible account, visit cph.org/podcast and listen to our Seeds of Faith podcast each week.

Preparing the Lesson © 2007, 2015 Concordia Publishing House. Scripture: ESV®.

Lesson 4

Joseph Forgives

Genesis 42–45; 50:15–21

Connections

Bible Words
Be kind . . . forgiving one another, as God in Christ forgave you. Ephesians 4:32

Faith Word
Forgive

Hymn
Lord Jesus, Think on Me (*LSB* 610; CD 1)

Catechism
Confession and Absolution

Liturgy
Confession and Absolution

Take-Home Promise
God forgives me and helps me forgive others.

1 Opening (15 minutes)

Welcome Time

What you do: Before class, set up two activity areas. In one, put out copies of Activity Page 4A and crayons or markers. Make copies of Activity Page Fun (below and on CD) for parents or classroom helpers.

In the other activity area, cover the table or floor with a large piece of newsprint, and draw the outline of a large cross on it. Set out glue sticks and Styrofoam packing peanuts, cotton balls, fabric scraps, uncooked macaroni, or paper to crumple (crumpling paper is good for fine-motor development).

Play the CD from your Teacher Tools. Greet each child at eye level.

Say **Hi, [Lydia]. How are you today? I wonder . . . what was a happy thing that happened to you this week? Today, you'll hear about some brothers who did a mean thing and what happened to make them happy.**

Direct children to the tables where you have the activities. Encourage parents or caregivers to stay and do the welcome activity with their child.

Activity Page Fun Get a copy of Activity Page 4A. Have your child describe what is happening in the picture.

Say **It is fun to celebrate a birthday, isn't it?** Have your child draw himself or herself by the gifts and color the page as you talk about times of celebration.

Ask **What are some other times our family gets together for a celebration?**

Say **Celebrations are happy times! Today, you will hear about a happy time when a brother forgives his brothers for being mean to him.**

MATERIALS NEEDED

1 Opening	2 God Speaks	3 We Live	4 Closing
Teacher Tools Attendance chart CD	**Teacher Tools** Poster B	**Student Pack** Craft Page 4 Stickers	**Student Pack** Take-home materials
Student Pack Attendance sticker	**Student Pack** Lesson Leaflet 4 Stickers	**Other Supplies** Sprout Straws & embellishments	
Other Supplies Activity Page 4A (TG) Newsprint & decorating supplies Resource Page 1 (TG, optional)	**Other Supplies** Sprout *Joseph: Jacob's Favorite Son* Arch Book (optional)	Sugar cookies & tubes of frosting or Jell-O jigglers Paper Plus supplies (optional)	

Active Learning Have the children use the materials you set out and work together to fill in the cross outline on the newsprint.

Ask **What does a cross remind you of?** Talk about how God forgives our sins because Jesus died on the cross for us.

Use your classroom signal to let the children know it's time to clean up and gather for circle time. Sing a cleanup song (Resource Page 1).

Gathering in God's Name

What you do: Having a routine can be very comforting for young children. Use this opening format each week so that children become familiar with it. To teach about the Church Year, use the materials in the Church Year Worship Kit (see the introduction for more information).

Sing "I Like to Be in Sunday School" (*LOSP*, p. 11; CD 14) or another opening song

Have the children say the Invocation and Amen with you. Tell them "Amen" is the special word they get to say at the end of prayers, hymns, and the like.

Begin **In the name of the Father and of the Son and of the Holy Spirit. Amen.**

Offering Have a child bring the offering basket forward. Sing an offering song.

Pray **Thank You, Jesus,* for making us Your children.* Forgive our sins.* Help us to listen* to Your Word* and learn more about You today.* For Jesus' sake we pray.* Amen.***

*Have children echo each phrase after you.

Celebrate Birthdays, Baptism birthdays, and special occasions

2 God Speaks (20 minutes)

Story Clue

What you do: Use Sprout or another puppet.

Teacher: Look girls and boys, it's our friend Sprout. Can you say hello to him? (*Children say hello and wave.*)

Sprout: (*Sounding glum*) Hi, Teacher. Hi, friends.

Teacher: What's wrong, Sprout? You sound sad.

Sprout: I am sad. And worried too. I think I'm in trouble because I knocked over a special picture frame from Grandma . . . and it broke.

Teacher: Oh. I see. What did your mom say, Sprout?

Sprout: I don't know. I ran out of the house before she found out. I didn't want her to know I did it. But I'm sure she'll be mad at me if she knows I did.

Teacher: You know, when I was little, something like this happened to me too.

Sprout: It did? What did you do?

Teacher: Well, it wasn't easy, but I told my mom I was sorry. And you know what she did? (*Sprout shakes head no.*) She came over and gave me a hug and said, "I forgive you."

Sprout: Really? Do you think my mom will forgive me if I did that?

Teacher: There's only one way to find out, Sprout.

Sprout: Yup. I better go find my mom and tell her I'm sorry. (*Putting head down, looking sad.*) But I'm afraid she'll be mad.

Teacher: It *is* hard to say we're sorry. But God will help you do that, Sprout. (*Put puppet away.*)

Say   Boys and girls, while Sprout goes to tell his mom he's sorry, let's listen to our Bible story. It's about some brothers who needed forgiveness.

Bible Story Time

What you do: Use Poster B to teach the Bible story. Open your Bible, and show children that today's story comes from Genesis 42–45; 50:15–21 in the Bible. Invite them to do the motions and sounds with you as you tell the story.

Say   Today's Bible story is from God's Word in the Book of Genesis. It is about Joseph and his brothers. It happened in two places: the land of Canaan, where Joseph's brothers lived, and the land of Egypt, where Joseph lived. For seven years, the people had lots of food to eat. Rub stomach. **But for the next seven years, there was a great famine.**

Ask   I wonder . . . what is a famine? Let children guess.

Say   Well, a famine is a time when people go hungry because there is hardly any food to eat. Make a sad face by using your fingers to turn down the corners of your mouth. **Joseph was an important person in Egypt now. The king of Egypt had put him in charge of the food. During the time when there was lots and lots of food, Joseph told the workers to put some of it in big barns. When no food would grow, Joseph gave the people some of the food that was saved in the barns so they weren't hungry.** Rub stomach.

Joseph's family lived far away in the land of Canaan, where there was no food. They were very hungry, so Joseph's brothers went to Egypt to buy food for the family. Clip, clop, clip, clop went the donkeys' feet as they went to Egypt. Clip, clop, clip, clop. Say clip clop, and step in place.

When they got there, they went to see the person in charge of the food. The brothers bowed down before him. Bend at waist with folded hands. **They asked him for some food. The brothers did not know they were bowing down and talking to their brother Joseph! But Joseph knew who his brothers were right away.**

He asked, "Do you have more people in your family?" The brothers said, "Yes, our youngest brother, Benjamin, is at home with our father."

Joseph said, "Bring me your brother." Then Joseph gave them some food and sent them home. Clip, clop, clip, clop went the donkeys' feet as they went back home. Clip, clop, clip, clop. Say clip clop, and step in place.

After some time, the family had eaten all the food they bought in Egypt. Rub stomach. **Their father, Jacob, said, "Go back to Egypt and buy more food." This time, Joseph's brothers took their youngest brother, Benjamin, with them. Clip, clop, clip, clop went the donkeys' feet as they went to Egypt.** Say clip clop, and step in place. **Clip, clop, clip, clop. They went to Joseph to buy more food. When Joseph saw Benjamin, he started to cry.** Show Poster B.

Then, Joseph's brothers had a big surprise! Joseph said, "I am Joseph!" Have children repeat, "I am Joseph!" with arms outstretched.

Instead of being happy, the brothers were afraid. They remembered that they had been mean to Joseph. Could this really be the Joseph they sold as a slave long ago? They thought Joseph would be angry with them and punish them. But Joseph said, "Don't be afraid. I forgive you." Then, Joseph hugged each of his brothers. Cross arms to hug self.

He told them, "Hurry and get my father. Tell him I am a ruler in Egypt. Bring him here so I can take care of all of you. You can live here and have enough to eat." So Joseph's father and brothers went to Egypt to live. They were one big, happy family again.

Joseph's brothers sinned when they were mean to Joseph. But God helped Joseph forgive his brothers. Later, Joseph told his brothers: "You meant evil against me, but God meant it for good so I could help many people." We think and say and do wrong things too. We sin. But God loves us. He forgives our sins for Jesus' sake and makes us part of His family through Baptism and His Word! He helps us forgive one another.

Bible Story Review

What you do: Show Poster B as you review the story. Then, hand out Lesson Leaflet 4, Jesus stickers, and crayons. *Option:* Review the story of Joseph's life with the Arch Book *Joseph: Jacob's Favorite Son* (CPH, 59-2233). Show the pictures, and have the children tell you what is happening.

Ask **What is happening in the picture?** Joseph is telling his brothers who he is.

How do his brothers feel when they hear it is Joseph? Scared, worried

What does Joseph tell them so they aren't afraid? I forgive you.

Who forgives you? Accept answers.

Hand out the leaflets, and point to the circles in the side box. Help the children find something for each color in the Bible story picture and circle it. Have them connect the dots on the cross and add a sticker of Jesus to it when you talk about the last question. Finish the review with the activity on the back of the leaflet.

Bible Words

What you do: Read the words from your Bible. Then, use the action rhyme to help the children learn the verse. Repeat several times.

Say	
Here is the Bible God gave me.	Open hands like a book.
What does He tell me?	Point to self.
Let's look and see.	Shade hands with hand.
In the Bible, God says:	Open hands like a book.
"Be kind . . .	Cross arms over heart.
forgiving one another,	Make a cross with fingers.
as God in Christ	Point up.
forgave you." Ephesians 4:32	Make a cross with fingers.

Teacher Tip

Try having that high-energy child be your special helper to hold a poster, hand out materials, and the like. Direct his or her energy in positive ways.

3 We Live (20 minutes)

Use these activities to help the children grow in their understanding of what the Bible story means for their lives. Choose the ones that work best with your class.

Growing through God's Word

What you do: Bring Sprout back.

Teacher: Hi, Sprout! How did it go with your mom?

Sprout: Great! I told my mom about breaking the picture, and I said I was sorry. My mom gave me a big hug and said, "I forgive you, Sprout."

Teacher: Oh, good, Sprout. I'm sure you feel better now.

Sprout: I sure do. I'm happy that my mom forgives me.

Teacher: Somebody else forgives us every day. Girls and boys, do you know who that is? (*Accept answers.*) Yes, it is God.

Sprout: Oh, I know, Teacher. It's like in church when we have the con . . . con . . .

Teacher: Confession?

Sprout: Right! Confession.

Teacher: You're right, Sprout. You said, "I'm sorry," to your mom when you broke her picture. In church, we confess our sins. We say, "I'm sorry," to God.

Sprout: My mom told me that she forgives me. Does God say, "I forgive you," too?

Teacher: He sure does. The pastor talks for God. He tells us, "I forgive you." We call this part the Absolution.

Sprout: Wow. That makes me happy to know that my mom *and* God forgive me!

Teacher: Being forgiven does make us happy. When Joseph forgave his brothers, they were happy too. Joseph gave his family a home in Egypt so they could all be together again and always have enough to eat.

Sprout: Hmmm. Food. That gives me an idea! I think I will go ask my mom for some ice cream!

Option: If you have time, role-play situations where the children can practice saying "I'm sorry" and "I forgive you." Talk about how God loves and forgives us for Jesus' sake and enables us to forgive others.

Craft Time

What you do: Hand out Craft Page 4, stickers, crayons, and two straws to each child. Provide embellishments, such as snippets of yarn, homemade confetti, or sequins. *Option:* Separate the flag pieces and attach straws before class.

Have children cut the two flags apart. Read "I am sorry" on the green flag.

Ask **When you've done something bad, you say, "I'm sorry." How do you feel when you say these words?** Accept answers.

Then, read "You are forgiven" on the blue flag.

Ask **How do you feel when you hear those words?** Accept answers.

Give children the face stickers. Tell them to put the sad face on the "I'm sorry" flag and the happy face on the "You are forgiven" flag.

Turn the flags over. Have the children connect the dots on the cross and heart. Give them crayons and other decorating supplies. Have them color the heart and cross and personalize their flags. Tell the children that the heart reminds us of God's love. The cross reminds us that God forgives us for Jesus' sake. He helps us to forgive others. Staple or tape straws to the flags.

Paper Plus option: Make copies of Activity 4B for children to make Baptism banners. Have paint smocks to cover Sunday clothing.

Help children add their name to the line. Give them sponges cut into cross shapes and paint to dab paint crosses onto their banners. When the crosses are dry, add yarn for hanging them. Talk about how God forgives our sins in Baptism.

Snack Time

What you do: Serve heart-shaped sugar cookies. Use tubes of icing to add crosses. Or make finger Jell-O jigglers (find recipe online) in the shape of crosses. Talk about how the cross reminds us of God's forgiveness.

Live It Out

Take a trip to the church sanctuary. Talk about the Confession and Absolution that we say in church. Have the children kneel and say "I'm sorry," or say this responsive prayer with them (adapted from *Wiggle & Wonder,* p. 13). Have children echo your words at the asterisks or just say the refrain.

Say   **Sometimes, I hug and help and clap.***
    Sometimes, I push and throw and slap.*
    Children: Jesus, I am sorry.* Please forgive me.*
    Sometimes, I am as helpful as can be.*
    Sometimes, I take things* that don't belong to me.*
    Children: Jesus, I am sorry.* Please forgive me.*
    Sometimes, I listen and obey.*
    Sometimes, I don't.* What can I say?*
    Children: Jesus, I am sorry.* Please forgive me.*
    When I sin, I'm sorry and so sad,*
    Jesus says, I forgive you,* and that makes me glad!*

Walk to the baptismal font and talk about how, through Baptism, God washes away our sins and tells us we are forgiven.

Encourage the children to say "I'm sorry" when they have done something bad this week and "I forgive you" to those who have wronged them.

 **4 Closing** (5 minutes)

Going Home

What you do: Have take-home materials ready to hand out. Give children their flags to wave as you say the take-home promise together.

Sing   "I Am Sorry, Jesus" (*LOSP,* p. 14) or "Lord Jesus, Think on Me" (*LSB* 610; CD 1)

Say   **Today, we learned that God forgives me and helps me forgive others. Let's say that together.** Say the take-home promise together.

Pray   **Dear God, thank You for forgiving us. Help us to show love and forgive others. For Jesus' sake, we pray. Amen.**

Reflection

Am I teaching at the right level for the children? Was anything too hard for them today? Was anything too easy? How can I adjust for next week?

name

God says, "I have called you by name, you are Mine."

Isaiah 43:1

Preparing the Lesson

The Birth of Moses

Exodus 1:1–2:10

Date of Use _____

Key Point

Through Moses, the Lord saved His people from slavery in Egypt. Through Christ, God saves all people from the bondage of sin and death.

Law/**Gospel**

In this world, I am enslaved by the demands of Satan. **God's Son, Jesus, was born to set me free from the slavery of sin, death, and the devil.**

Context

God declared to Abraham that his descendants would "be sojourners in a land that is not theirs and will be servants there, and they will be afflicted for four hundred years" (Genesis 15:13).

Since Joseph had saved Egypt from famine, four hundred years of bondage to Egypt proved to be God's true prophetic Word for His people. The birth of Moses is the beginning of the fulfillment of God's promise to Abraham that afterward, Israel would "come out with great possessions" (Genesis 15:14).

Commentary

"I'm beat!" We all utter this expression from time to time. It is a simple way to say we are tired, busy, and overwhelmed by the forces of this fallen world and our own sinful flesh. Without relief, we easily become consumed by worry. Our despair at bitter tasks can lead us to unbelief.

Israel was "beat." By the time of Moses' birth, the fruition of God's dire prediction of four hundred years of servitude is evident. God's promise to Abraham of relief must have seemed small and remote compared with the sore backs and calloused hands that bricks, mortar, and forced labor produced. Pharaoh's decree to have all of the sons of Israel killed at birth must have left Israel debilitated in their despair.

Into this world of pessimism, God delivers a son from the house of Levi. Through divine guidance, the midwives defy the death command, and the baby floats downriver to become a son of the household of Pharaoh himself. In this child, the Lord has now provided for His people hope of salvation from their servitude.

Likewise, God declares, "Out of Egypt I called My Son" (Matthew 2:15). In spite of a similar death sentence from Herod, a Hebrew maidservant delivered the Son of God, Jesus Christ. Under the watchful eyes of this new Miriam, Jesus would sail into the hands of the house of pharaoh, the devil himself, where He would suffer the bitterest toil for us. On His back, He would carry the rigors of our servitude to sin all the way to Golgotha. Our Savior would rescue more than the Hebrews. He would free all nations from the bitter toil of our sins and leave the world "beat."

In His Word, Christ breathes healing back into our sin-enslaved souls. In His Word, He proclaims to us, "Come to Me, all who labor and are heavy laden, and I will give you rest" (Matthew 11:28). May we continue to hear the voice of our new and better Moses, the sweet Word of our gentle and lowly Servant, who gives rest for our weary souls.

To hear an in-depth discussion of this Bible account, visit cph.org/podcast and listen to our Seeds of Faith podcast each week.

Preparing the Lesson © 2007, 2015 Concordia Publishing House. Scripture: ESV®.

Lesson 5

The Birth of Moses

Exodus 1:1–2:10

Connections

Bible Words
[God] cares for you. 1 Peter 5:7

Faith Word
Save

Hymn
Lord Jesus, Think on Me
(*LSB* 610; CD 1)

Catechism
Apostles' Creed:
First and Second Articles

Take-Home Promise
God cares for me.

1 Opening (15 minutes)

Welcome Time

What you do: Before class, set up two activity areas. In one, put out copies of Activity Page 5 and crayons or markers. Make copies of Activity Page Fun (below and on CD) for parents or classroom helpers.

In the other activity area, set a tub of rice on a towel. (The towel will catch rice spills, making for easier cleanup.) Hide objects in the rice for the children to discover. Alternately, set out baby dolls and baby care items such as bottles, blankets, bath items, toy dishes, spoons, and bibs.

Play the CD from your Teacher Tools. Greet each child at eye level. Set out a variety of baby pictures, or create a short video of babies sleeping, eating, crying, being played with, and the like. Show this as children enter.

Say Hi, [Nicholas]. Good to see you! Today, we're going to hear about a special baby in the Bible. I wonder . . . what can babies do by themselves? What do they need someone to do for them?

Let children share; then, help them get involved in an activity. Encourage parents or caregivers to stay and do the welcome activity with their child.

Activity Page Fun Get a copy of Activity Page 5. Show it to your child. Have your child circle the things we use to care for a baby, and then color the page.

Say In our Bible story today, you will hear about how God took care of a very special baby named Moses. Listen, so you can tell me about it later.

MATERIALS NEEDED

1 Opening	2 God Speaks	3 We Live	4 Closing
Teacher Tools Attendance chart CD	**Teacher Tools** Storytelling Figures 5-1 to 5-7 Background B	**Teacher Tools** Storytelling Figures 5-3 & 5-5 Poster C	**Teacher Tools** CD
Student Pack Attendance sticker	**Student Pack** Lesson Leaflet 5 & sticker	**Student Pack** Craft Page 5 Stickers	**Student Pack** Take-home materials
Other Supplies Activity Page 5 (TG) Tub of rice with hidden objects & towel, or dolls & baby-care items Resource Page 1 (TG)	**Other Supplies** Baskets Pan of water, play dough & craft sticks; cup; green chenille stems or yarn (optional) *Tiny Baby Moses* Arch Book (optional)	**Other Supplies** Basket Celery & toppings Raffia or twine & fabric (optional) Paper Plus supplies (optional)	

44

Active Learning Encourage children to look for objects hiding in the rice. If you set out baby dolls and baby-care items, have the children pretend to care for the babies.

Say **Today, you will hear how a family hid their baby in a basket on the river to save him from a bad ruler.**

Use your classroom signal to let the children know it's time to clean up and gather for circle time. Sing a cleanup song (Resource Page 1).

Gathering in God's Name

What you do: Gather the children, and begin with this opening. To teach about the Church Year, use the materials in the Church Year Worship Kit (see the introduction for more information).

Sing "I Like to Be in Sunday School" (*LOSP*, p. 11; CD 14) or another opening song

Have the children say the Invocation and Amen with you. Tell them "Amen" is the special word they get to say at the end of prayers, hymns, and the like.

Begin **In the name of the Father and of the Son and of the Holy Spirit. Amen.**

Offering Have a child bring the offering basket forward. Sing an offering song.

Pray **Dear God,* thank You for caring for us* and keeping us safe.* Thank You for sending Jesus* to be our Savior.* Help us to listen* and learn* more about You* in Sunday School today.* Amen.***

*Have children echo each phrase after you.

Celebrate Birthdays, Baptism birthdays, and special occasions

2 God Speaks (20 minutes)

Story Clue

What you do: Bring several different types of baskets to talk about. Show baskets one at a time and discuss their uses.

Ask **What is this? What can you use this basket for?** Accept responses. **If we put this basket in water, will it sink or float?** Accept answers.

Say **In our Bible story today, a bad king wanted to hurt all the baby boys that belonged to God's people. But one baby's mother made a special basket for her baby. She used it to keep her baby safe. Let's listen to our Bible story and find out what happened.**

Bible Story Time

What you do: Use Storytelling Figures 5-1 to 5-7 and Background B. For extra impact, fill a shallow pan with water to use as the river. Set the background behind the water. Attach your figures to craft sticks, and put them in play-dough bases. Place them near the water as you tell the story. Attach baby Moses to half a Styrofoam cup so he floats.

Option: Show the pictures and tell the story of Moses using the Arch Book *Tiny Baby Moses* (CPH, 59-1550).

Say   Many years ago, God's people, the Israelites, lived in a country called Egypt. The ruler of the country was called a pharaoh. Pharaoh was a bad king. He made God's people his slaves and was mean to them. He made them work extra hard. Pharaoh was afraid of God's people because there were so many of them. So, he made a law that said, "Every baby boy that is born in an Israelite family should be killed."

Ask   Was this a good law?

Say   No, it was a bad law! We should never hurt babies! But God loved His people. He had a special plan to save them. One day, He sent a special baby to one family. Show baby (1-1). **God planned for this baby to grow up and save His people.**

How happy the baby's family was when he was born! His mother loved her baby boy very much. His father loved him. His big brother and big sister loved him! They did not want him to be hurt. They did not obey the bad law. Instead, the baby's family hid him for three months so the bad king's soldiers could not hurt him. But the baby kept growing and growing. Soon, he was too big and noisy to hide anymore!

God helped the baby's mother think of a way to save her baby. First, she made a basket that would float on the water. Then, she put her baby inside the basket and covered him with some warm blankets. She hurried to the river and hid the basket in the tall grass near the edge of the water. Replace 5-1 with Moses in basket (5-2). **Then, she told the baby's big sister, Miriam, to hide near the baby and make sure he was safe.** Add figure 5-3.

Soon, Miriam heard some footsteps! Oh, no. Who was coming? Would God keep her baby brother safe? Then, Miriam saw a princess walking toward the river with her servants. Add servants (5-4) and princess (5-5). **The princess was Pharaoh's daughter. She was going to have a bath in the water. The princess saw the little basket in the grassy water and sent one of her servants to get it.** Replace 5-4 with kneeling servant (5-6). **When the princess uncovered the basket, there was the little baby boy. The princess took the baby out of his basket.** Remove figures; add princess holding baby (5-6).

"Oh! He's so sweet. He must be one of the Israelite babies," she said. The princess knew about the law, but she didn't want the baby to be hurt. She said, "I will keep this baby for myself. I will name him Moses because I took him out of the water. He will be my son."

The baby's sister, Miriam, heard what the princess said. Point to Miriam (5-3). **She ran up and asked, "Would you like me to get an Israelite woman to take care of the baby for you?"**

"Yes," said the princess. So, Miriam ran home as fast as she could and brought her mother to the princess. Remove Miriam. **Moses' own mother got to take care of him for the princess.**

Moses' mother was happy. She loved her baby. She fed him and took good care of him. When he was older, she took him back to the princess. Then, Moses lived in the king's palace until he was grown.

God loved Moses. He sent many people to care for Moses and keep him safe. He had a special job for Moses to do. God planned for Moses to

Key Point

In Moses, the Lord saved His people from slavery in Egypt. In Christ, God saves all people from the bondage of sin and death.

grow up and help His people get away from mean Pharaoh. God wanted to keep His people safe so that many years later, His Son, Jesus, could be born. God loves you and cares for you too. He loves you so much that He sent Jesus to be your Savior.

Bible Story Review

What you do: Hand out Lesson Leaflet 5 and crayons. To provide a tactile element, supply green chenille stems or yarn and glue sticks. Draw children's attention to the leaflet picture.

Ask **Who is the baby in the basket?** Moses

Who are the other people? Miriam, the princess, and servants

How did God keep Moses safe? He worked through his mother, who made a basket to hide him in; through his sister, who watched over him in the river; and through the princess, who took him as her son.

How does God care for you? Accept answers.

Do the sidebar activity on the front of the leaflet. Give the children green chenille stems or yarn to glue to the reeds on side 2 for a three-dimensional look.

Have children stand up and pretend to rock a baby in their arms. Sing the following to the tune of "Rock-a-bye Baby."

Sing **Rock-a-bye Moses in your safe spot.**
God will protect you; He loves you a lot!
God's got a plan. We know He'll come through.
So don't be afraid; He'll watch over you.

Option: Give the children an opportunity to stretch by having them act out a family activity (e.g., sweeping the floor, washing dishes, folding clothes). Give each child a turn at being the leader. Talk about God's care for us through our families.

Bible Words

What you do: Have your Bible open to 1 Peter 5:7. You will also need the stickers that say "God cares for me!"

Say **The Bible tells us "[God] cares for you." Today, we learned about Moses and how God cared for him. God loves you and cares for you too. I have a sticker for you today. It has a big heart that says "God cares for me!"**

Ask **What else do you see on the sticker?** A cross

Say **This heart and cross remind us of God's love and care. Our biggest trouble is our sin—the bad things we say and do. But God loves us. He took care of our sin trouble by sending Jesus to die on the cross for us. You can wear the sticker on your shirt to remind you that "[God] cares for you." Let's say our Bible Words rhyme with our Bible Words.**

Say **Here is the Bible God gave me.**   Open hands like a book.
What does He tell me?   Point to self.
Let's look and see.   Shade hands with hand.
The Bible says: Open hands like a book.
"[God] cares for you."   Point up, hug self, point to others.

3 We Live (20 minutes)

Use these activities to help the children grow in their understanding of what the Bible story means for their lives. Choose the ones that work best with your class.

Growing through God's Word

What you do: Cut apart the figures on Poster C. You will also need the story figures of Miriam (5-3) and the princess (5-7). Put them all in a basket with the figures of the princess, Miriam, and Moses' mother on top.

Say   God loved baby Moses very much. How did God take care of him?

Remove figures from basket one at a time, and comment on each one.

Say   God gave Moses a family to love and take care of him. Show mother. **How did Moses' mother care for Moses?** (She made a basket to keep him safe.) Show sister (5-3). **What did Moses' sister do for Moses?** (She watched over him when he was in the water.) Show princess (5-7). **How did God use the princess to care for Moses?** (She took Moses to be her son.)

God loves us and takes care of us too. One way He cares for us and keeps us safe is by giving us a family. Show the work man or another man figure. **Who is this? What are some ways daddies care for us?** Accept comments. Show grandma. **Who could this be? How do grandmas care for us? Who else is in your family? How do they care for you? God also gives us other people to care for us.**

One at a time, show the remaining figures (teacher, doctor, pastor, and policeman or work man) as you ask how God cares for us through each one. Finally, show the Jesus figure.

Say   The very best way God cares for us is by giving us Jesus, our Savior! Because Jesus came to die for us, God forgives our sins. Because of Jesus, God promises that He will always take care of us. That makes me feel thankful. Let's tell God how we feel. Have children bow heads and fold hands as you pray.

Pray   Dear God, thank You for saving me. Thank You for loving me and taking care of me. Help me to trust in You. Amen.

Craft Time

What you do: Hand out Craft Page 5 and the stickers from the Sticker Page. *Option:* Supply strips of raffia or twine and small squares of fabric for a baby blanket.

Children will cut off the strip with baby, then color the water and the princess's clothes. Give them jewelry stickers for the princess. For a tactile component, give the children pieces of raffia or twine to glue to the basket and a fabric blanket for Moses.

As the children complete each piece, cut around baby Moses in his basket and the princess. Glue baby Moses on the arms of the princess so that she is holding the baby. To finish, tape the sides of the base so the princess will stand up.

Say   God took care of Moses and kept him safe. Who is holding baby Moses?

Teacher Tip

Give the children glue sticks, or put a small amount of glue on plastic lids and have the children use small paintbrushes or cotton Q-tips to transfer the glue. For younger children and those who have fine-motor delays, put the glue on the project for them; have them add the raffia or twine.

Growing in CHRIST.

How did God use the princess to take care of Moses? God gives us people to take care of us too. Who takes care of you? What do they do for you?

Paper Plus option: Make baby Moses dolls. You will need a white tube sock for each child, rubber bands or yarn, a permanent marker, cotton batting or fiberfill to stuff the socks, squares of fabric for baby blankets, and lunch-size paper bags.

Help the children draw smiling faces on the toe side of their sock. Fill the socks with batting or fiberfill, and close with rubber bands or tie with yarn. Have children select a fabric sample and wrap their baby Moses in the cloth. Cut the tops off the paper bags so that the bag is only about one-third as tall as the original height. Place baby Moses inside for an instant "basket."

Snack Time

What you do: Serve celery filled with pressurized cheese or dates stuffed with flavored cream cheese. Talk about how the snack reminds you of Moses' little basket.

Live It Out

Have children bring items (e.g., diapers, onesies, bibs, formula) to make baby-care baskets for a local crisis pregnancy center to give out to moms in need.

4 Closing (5 minutes)

Going Home

What you do: Gather children's take-home items to hand out.

Sing "God Is So Good" (*LOSP*, p. 57; CD 8) or "Lord Jesus, Think on Me" (*LSB* 610; CD 1)

Say **God cared for baby Moses and kept him safe. God cares for us too. The very best way God cares for us is by sending Jesus to save us from our sins.**

Lead children in saying "God cares for me" after each line you say (adapted from *Fingers Tell the Story*, p. 81). Conclude with a prayer of thanks.

Say **In the morning, I wake up and say,**

Children: God cares for me.

God will be with me all through the day.

Children: God cares for me.

God gives me food, clothing, and friends.

Children: God cares for me.

His love for me will never end.

Children: God cares for me.

Reflection

Were the children able to talk about how God cares for them? In future weeks, how can you continue to make the connection for them between God caring for baby Moses and God caring for us by sending Jesus to be our Savior?

Lesson 5

Circle and color all the things that we use to take care of babies.

Preparing the Lesson

Moses and the Burning Bush

Exodus 2:11–4:31

Date of Use _____

Key Point

As God had Moses remove the sandals from his feet, God, in Christ, removes our sins from us, making us fit to approach God and stand in His presence.

Law/**Gospel**

Because of sin, I cannot approach the Lord. **Christ removes my sin so that I am declared blameless before God.**

Context

Moses kills an Egyptian who is beating a Hebrew servant. Moses flees to Midian. In so doing, Moses chooses "rather to be mistreated with the people of God than to enjoy the fleeting pleasures of sin. He considered the reproach of Christ greater wealth than the treasures of Egypt" (Hebrews 11:25–26). In the form of a burning bush, God reveals to Moses that He will deliver Israel into a thorn-free land "flowing with milk and honey" (Exodus 3:8).

Commentary

We all want to be accepted and loved exactly "as we are." God says, "Cursed is the ground because of you; . . . thorns and thistles it shall bring forth for you" (Genesis 3:17–18). On account of our sin, God removes us from His holy presence in His first Eden and clothes our shameful bodies. Our sin, our being "as we are," places us in a more fitting land, where the very ground produces thorns and thistles.

In our accursed land, Moses shepherds his flock. Of all humanity, God might at least accept His chosen Moses just "as he is." Yet God says, "Take your sandals off your feet, for the place on which you are standing is holy ground" (Exodus 3:5). God alone is holy. God abhors anything less in His presence. Moses cannot come "as he is." He must leave behind the reminder of our first clothing and resulting expulsion from Eden, even his sandals.

Nevertheless, who can approach the Lord without downcast eyes? We cannot "as we are." We cannot without God's only Son. Thanks be to God that Jesus Christ has taken the very form of our curse, the thorns and thistles of our cursed ground.

Even more so, the same God who shows Himself to Moses in the burning bush appears again on a new and deadlier tree. Again, He adorns His head in a crown of thorns. On this tree, He removes the effects of the curse from us forever. The thorns and nails of that tree cannot extinguish the burning yet unconsumed light of the world! Indeed, He perseveres even unto death and rises again so that we might know that by His becoming our curse, we are now eternally blessed.

During the Divine Service, we see God loving us because of the thorn-encrusted head of His Son. He beckons us to approach Him and confess our sins, and the great I AM forgives our sins in Absolution on account of Christ's thorn-pierced brow. The Lord removes these sins from us even as He removed Moses' sandals from his feet. In Absolution, God accepts us not "as we are," but for who Jesus is and what He did on Calvary for us. May the Lord continue to direct us to Confession and Absolution so that we may receive the curse-removing love of our Savior, Jesus Christ.

To hear an in-depth discussion of this Bible account, visit cph.org/podcast and listen to our Seeds of Faith podcast each week.

Lesson 6

Moses and the Burning Bush

Exodus 2:11–4:31

Connections

Bible Words
[God says,] "I have chosen you . . . ; fear not, for I am with you." Isaiah 41:9–10

Faith Word
Holy

Hymn
Lord Jesus, Think on Me
(*LSB* 610; CD 1)

Catechism
Apostles' Creed:
Second Article

Liturgy
Invocation

Take-Home Promise
God takes away my sin and calls me to serve Him.

1 Opening (15 minutes)

Welcome Time

What you do: Before class, set up two activity areas. In one, put out copies of Activity Page 6, crayons or markers, cotton balls and glue sticks. Make copies of Activity Page Fun (below and on CD) for parents or classroom helpers.

In the other activity area, set out a variety of Bibles and Bible story books for the children to examine. Include *The Story Bible* (CPH, 01-2049), which has the same realistic pictures of the Bible stories as the children's leaflets.

Say Hi, [Lucy]. It's good to see you here! I wonder . . . does your [grandma] live near or far away? How does she talk to you? Today you'll hear how God talked to Moses.

Direct children to the tables where you have the activities. Encourage parents or caregivers to stay and do the welcome activity with their child.

Activity Page Fun Get a copy of Activity Page 6. Work with your child to color the page and glue pieces of pulled-apart cotton balls to the sheep.

Ask What is this animal? Who is the person taking care of the sheep?

Say Shepherds have important jobs. They make sure their sheep have food and water. They keep their sheep safe. In the Bible story today, Moses is a shepherd, but God has another important job for Moses to do. Listen to find out what it is.

© 2015 Concordia Publishing House. Reproduced by permission. Available on the Teacher CD.

MATERIALS NEEDED

1 Opening	2 God Speaks	3 We Live	4 Closing
Teacher Tools Attendance chart CD	**Teacher Tools** Poster D	**Student Pack** Craft Page 6 Stickers	**Student Pack** Take-home materials CD
Student Pack Attendance sticker	**Student Pack** Lesson Leaflet 6 Sticker	**Other Supplies** Story bag with candle, lighter, Bible & shell	
Other Supplies Activity Page 6 (TG) Cotton balls Bibles & Bible story books Resource Page 1 (TG)	**Other Supplies** Story bag Cell or toy phone Large piece of construction paper Picture of a snake	Stick pretzels & fruit roll-ups Yarn (optional) Hole punch (optional) Paper Plus supplies (optional)	

Active Learning Encourage the children to examine the Bibles and storybooks.

Say **These books help us learn about God.** Point to the Bibles. **The words in these books are God's exact words to us. When we listen to the Bible, we are listening to God talking to us.**

Use your classroom signal to let the children know it's time to clean up and gather for circle time. Sing a cleanup song (Resource Page 1).

Gathering in God's Name

What you do: Gather the children and begin with this opening. To teach about the Church Year, use the materials in the Church Year Worship Kit (see the introduction for more information).

Sing "I Like to Be in Sunday School" (*LOSP*, p. 11; CD 14) or another opening song

Say **This is a special place because our awesome and holy God is here with us! On our own, we don't deserve to be near Him, because we think and say and do bad things. But God has taken away our sin through Jesus and made us His children through Baptism and His Word. Because we are His children, we can call on His name.**

Have the children say the Invocation and Amen with you.

Begin **In the name of the Father and of the Son and of the Holy Spirit. Amen.**

Offering Have a child bring the offering basket forward. Sing an offering song.

Pray **Dear God,* thank You* for taking away our sins* through Jesus* and for calling us* through Baptism and Your Word* to be Your children.* Help us to listen and learn* more about You* in Sunday School today.* Amen.***

*Have children echo each phrase after you.

Celebrate Birthdays, Baptism birthdays, and special occasions

2 God Speaks (20 minutes)

Story Clue

What you do: Put your cell phone or a toy phone in your story bag.

Say **Good morning, boys and girls. Before we begin, I need to talk to Sprout. He isn't here today. I have something in my story bag that will help me get in touch with him, though. What do you think it is?** Accept answers.

Yes, it's a phone! Let's see if I can talk to him now. Pretend to phone Sprout. **Hello? Hi, Sprout.** Listen. **I'm sorry you are sick in bed! I hope you feel better soon. I just wanted to let you know we miss you here at Sunday School. I'll send your lesson to you in the mail. . . . Okay. I hope we see you next Sunday. Good-bye!** Put phone down. **Sprout was happy to hear from me. He says hello to all of you.**

Ask **Do you ever talk to anyone on the phone? Who?** Accept answers.

Say **We use phones to talk to people when we can't see them. In our Bible story today, God wanted to talk to Moses. But He didn't use a phone! He used something else—something bright and hot!**

Key Point

Just as God had Moses remove the sandals from his feet, God, in Christ, removes our sins from us, making us fit to approach God and stand in His presence.

Teacher Tip

A child who is inattentive or fidgety may be a kinesthetic learner (one who learns best through touch and hands-on activities). Provide soft objects to correspond to the Bible story (i.e., a lamb) or textured fabric squares (felt, velour, fake fur) to hold during sitting times for a calming effect.

Bible Story Time

What you do: Use a child's colored Activity Page 6, Poster D, a large piece of construction paper, and loops of tape or a restickable glue stick. Also, find a picture of a snake online or one in a storybook to show.

To prepare the construction paper, fold it in half and then half again to make four rectangles. Cut it apart on the fold lines. Tape the four sections over Poster D. As you tell the story, remove the designated piece of paper covering the poster, revealing more and more of the story. This will help the children focus on each part of the story better, keeping the rest as a surprise.

Have your Bible open. Tell children that you have a surprise picture to show them as you tell them this true story from God's Word.

Say **God took care of baby Moses and kept him safe. When Moses grew up, he became a shepherd. Moses took care of sheep for his family.** Show Activity Page 6. Comment on how you liked the way the children colored a page like this today and thank [Stella] for letting you borrow hers.

One day, Moses went to look for food and water for his sheep at a new place. This place was near a mountain. All of a sudden, Moses saw a bush that was on fire! Show Poster D, removing the piece of paper on the upper right corner to reveal the burning bush.

Moses walked closer. He watched the fire burning in the bush. But He saw that the bush did not burn up! What a strange thing, thought Moses. Then Moses heard someone calling his name. "Moses! Moses!" It was God, talking to him from the burning bush!

"Here I am," Moses answered.

Then God said, "Don't come any closer. This is a special place. Take off your sandals. You are standing on holy ground."

Moses took off his sandals. Remove the piece of paper covering the bottom right corner. Ask for a volunteer to point to the sandals.

Then God told him, "I am the Lord, your God, the God of your fathers." Moses put his hands in front of his face because he was afraid. Remove paper on top left corner.

God said, "I have seen the troubles of My people in Egypt. I have heard them praying because people are mean to them. I want you to lead My people out of Egypt. I want you to take them to a new, safe land where they will be happy."

But Moses was afraid. He asked, "How can I do such a hard job by myself? No one will believe that You sent me."

God promised Moses that He would be with him and help him. God wanted Moses to know He would give him power to do the job. So, God said, "Throw your shepherd's staff on the ground." Remove the last piece of paper and run your finger from top to bottom along the staff in Moses' hand. **Moses threw the staff down, and he got a big surprise.**

Ask **What do you think it was?** Accept guesses.

Say **The staff became a snake!** Show picture of a snake.

Say **Then God told Moses to catch the snake by its tail. When Moses did, it became his shepherd's staff again.** Point to the staff on the poster. **God**

did more things to show Moses that He would be with him. Still, Moses was afraid. He didn't think he could do the job God wanted him to do.

Finally, God promised Moses a helper. He told Moses that his brother, Aaron, would go with him and help him. Together, Moses and Aaron went to God's people, the Israelites, and told them what happened. They showed them God's signs. Then the people believed that God wanted to save them. They bowed their heads and worshiped God.

God talked to Moses from the burning bush and gave him a special job. He promised to be with Moses, and He gave him special signs to show that He would give Moses power to do this job. He gave Moses a helper.

God takes away our sin for Jesus' sake. He calls us by name in Baptism and makes us holy. He talks to us in His Word and gives us power to live as His children and serve in His kingdom.

Bible Story Review

What you do: Show Poster D and use the questions to review the story. Hand out Leaflet 6, the Bible sticker, and crayons or markers. *Option:* Do the action rhyme "Moses and the Burning Bush" (*Wiggle & Wonder*, p. 51; CPH, 22-3130).

Ask   **What is happening in the picture?** Accept answers.

What does God want Moses to do? He tells him to take off his sandals; He wants Moses to lead His people out of Egypt.

How does God talk to you? God talks to us in His Word.

On side 1 of the leaflets, have the children circle the correct answer in the sidebar. Give them a Bible sticker to put under the question. On side 2, have them color the burning bush. *Option:* Have the children sit in a circle and play Telephone. Whisper "Moses" or "Take off your sandals" to the first child. Have that child whisper it to the next one, and so on. After the game, review how God talked to Moses from the burning bush and how He talks to us through His Word.

Bible Words

What you do: Open your Bible to Isaiah 41:9–10 and read the words from there.

Say   In the Bible [God says,] "I have chosen you . . . ; fear not, for I am with you." God chose Moses to do a special job for Him. Moses was afraid, but God promised to be with Moses and help him do what He wanted.

God has chosen each of you to be His child through Baptism and His Word. He forgives you and gives you power to serve Him.

Ask   **What are some of the things God wants you to do?** Accept answers, such as showing love for others, being kind, obeying parents, telling about Jesus.

Say   Sometimes we may think we can't do what God wants us to do. Sometimes we sin and do just the opposite. Then we may be afraid that God or others don't love us. But God loves us so much that He sent Jesus to be our Savior. So, whenever you are afraid, remember our Bible words: [God says,] "I have chosen you . . . ; fear not, for I am with you." Let's say them to our neighbor. Divide children into two groups. Have the first group say the first half. Have the second group respond with the second half.

Group 1: [God says,] "I have chosen you . . . ;

Group 2: fear not, for I am with you."

Option: Play Telephone again. This time, whisper the first half of the verse to the first child and go clockwise around the circle. Then reverse directions. Begin with the last child and say the second half of the verse, going counterclockwise.

3 We Live (20 minutes)

Use these activities to help the children grow in their understanding of what the Bible story means for their lives. Choose the ones that work best with your class.

Growing through God's Word

What you do: Put a candle and lighter, a Bible, and a shell in your story bag (or enlarge the one here to show the children). *Option:* Take your children into church. Point out the altar candles, Bible, and baptismal font.

Say Earlier, I had a telephone in my story bag. We use a phone to talk to people we can't see. But God didn't talk on a telephone, did He? I have something in my story bag to remind us of how God talked to Moses.

Ask What do you think it is? Take out candle, and light it. **Can you see the fire?**

Say Our candle is burning. God spoke from the burning bush. He was right there with Moses! We light candles at the beginning of our church service to show that God is with us too. We begin in His name. Say the Invocation. In church, we are on holy ground because God is there, and God is holy. *Holy* means God never does anything bad. He never sins.

Ask Where do we hear our holy God talking to us? Take out the Bible.

Say God talks to us in His Word, the Bible! He tells us that He sent Jesus to die on the cross for us. Point to the baptismal font or hold up a shell. **God calls us by name in our Baptism and makes us His children. He forgives our sins for Jesus' sake.**

God gave Moses a job to do and promised to be with him. He gave Moses a staff that would become a snake. This staff was a sign of God's power. He gave Moses a helper, his brother Aaron. God calls you to be His child and serve Him too. He takes away your sin. He gives you His love in His Word and Baptism. He gives you parents and pastors and teachers to help you learn about Jesus and live as His child. He gives you ways to serve Him by serving others.

Ask What are some ways you can serve today? Help children think about ways they can serve God by showing love to others, and so forth.

Craft Time

What you do: You will need Craft Page 6, the stickers from the Sticker Page, and crayons or markers. *Option:* Supply two pieces of yarn per child to lace through the holes of the sandals. Fold page on lines so only the sandals show.

Ask What do these look like? (Sandals)

Have children color the sandals. *Option:* Punch holes at the dots, and help them lace a length of yarn through the holes in each sandal so the ends can be tied on top.

Ask What did God tell Moses? (Take off your sandals.) Open page.

Preparing the Lesson

Moses and the Plagues

Exodus 5–10

Date of Use

Key Point

Through a series of horrific plagues, God punished the Egyptians for their sinful treatment of God's people and freed His people from bondage. Through His horrific suffering and death on the cross, Jesus takes the punishment for our sin and frees us from sin's bondage.

Law/**Gospel**

On my own, I see no need for God in my life or in the world. **Christ suffered and died on the cross to free me from the bondage of sin, enabling me to see that He is the one I need most in this world.**

Context

Moses returns to Egypt to speak God's words to Pharaoh: "Let My people go" (Exodus 5:1). God inflicts ten plagues upon Egypt, but Pharaoh hardens his heart and refuses to let the Hebrews go.

Commentary

We know our birth dates. We know our favorite sports teams and musicians. We know every desire that can be described as "ours." Yet do we know the Lord God, whose speaking brings about amazing miracles?

Pharaoh does not know the Lord. At the coming of Moses, many gods are vying for legitimacy in Pharaoh's land. After four hundred years of Israel's oppression, the Lord introduces Himself. In the hand of Moses, God's staff-turned-snake devours the staffs of false gods. God's staff turns the waters of Egypt into blood. Frogs, gnats, flies, disease, boils, hail and fire from heaven, locusts, and three days of darkness leave Egypt in shambles. Even with God Himself speaking to Pharaoh, Pharaoh's heart continually hardens to the reality of the Lord's existence.

Without a miracle, our "Pharaoh-flesh" hardens to the reality of the Lord's existence. Astonishingly, God does not content Himself with our desires. God multiplies His signs so His "name may be proclaimed in all the earth" (Exodus 9:16).

"All the earth" is Pharaoh. "All the earth" is us too! God acts to redeem all people. Egypt receives the bloody rivers, famines, and darkened days of God's "wake-up call" so that the Lord might pull all the earth out of unbelief and into knowledge of Him as uniquely God.

In the ten plagues of Egypt, God spoke to His people of old. "But in these last days He has spoken to us by His Son" (Hebrews 1:2). However, God's language is the same. He speaks deliverance for His people through miraculous signs.

As the casting of Aaron's staff causes the plagues of Egypt, so Christ's cross punishes our Disease-bearer for the pestilences of our hardened hearts. As the rivers of Egypt ran red with supernatural blood, so the outpouring of Christ's blood shatters our inward gazing and lifts our eyes to behold the plague of hardness being purged from our hearts. For three hours, Christ suffered utter darkness on Calvary. Thus, the Lord introduces Himself to the world as her Savior. In Christ's cross, we know God as He is. His indefatigable love is for us all.

Through the retelling of Christ's plague-ridden crucifixion, the Lord shatters the walls of our hardened hearts. He produces faith that God not only justly punished our self-idolatry on Calvary, but also loves us so much that He invites us to know Him as He is—pure mercy. This knowledge of God's love in His Son fashions us as His new Israel and brings us from servitude into His heavenly kingdom.

To hear an in-depth discussion of this Bible account, visit cph.org/podcast and listen to our Seeds of Faith podcast each week.

Lesson 7

Moses and the Plagues
Exodus 5–10

Connections

Bible Words
God is our . . . help in trouble. Psalm 46:1 (CD 5)

Faith Word
Deliver

Hymn
Lord Jesus, Think on Me
(*LSB* 610; CD 1)

Catechism
Lord's Prayer: Seventh Petition

Take-Home Promise
God delivers me from sin and evil through Jesus.

1 Opening (15 minutes)

Welcome Time

What you do: Before class, set up two activity areas to provide a connection from what children know to what they will learn in the Bible lesson. In one, put out copies of Activity Page 7A and crayons or markers. Make copies of Activity Page Fun (below and on CD) for parents or classroom helpers.

In the other activity area, set out blocks, toy people, and rescue vehicles such as fire trucks, police cars, and ambulances.

Say Hi, [Liam]. It's good to see you here! I wonder . . . what is your favorite animal? Today we'll talk about some animals and insects in the Bible and also about God's power.

Direct children to the tables where you have the activities. Encourage parents or caregivers to stay and do the welcome activity with their child.

Activity Page Fun Get a copy of Activity Page 7A. Show it to your child. Point to the people (and cat) in the picture who need to be rescued from trouble. Talk about how they need someone to help rescue, or deliver, them.

Say This girl is afraid of the turkey. Who will help her? Let your child tell. **The boy is lost in the maze. Who will help him?** Let your child tell. **We call someone who rescues us from trouble a deliverer. The Bible tells us about a time when God heard the prayers of His people and made a rescue plan to deliver them from mean Pharaoh. God had a rescue plan for us too. The hidden crosses in the picture are a clue. How many can you find?**

MATERIALS NEEDED

1 Opening	2 God Speaks	3 We Live	4 Closing
Teacher Tools Attendance chart CD	**Teacher Tools** Storytelling Figures 7-1 to 7-14 Background B	**Teacher Tools** Storytelling Figures 7-1 Poster E	**Teacher Tools** CD
Student Pack Attendance sticker	**Student Pack** Lesson Leaflet 7	**Student Pack** Craft Page 7 Stickers	**Student Pack** Take-home materials
Other Supplies Activity Page 7A (TG) Blocks, toy people & rescue vehicles Resource Page 1 (TG)	**Other Supplies** Sprout Story bag Action figures or superhero pictures Pictures of pyramids (optional) Black paper (optional) Towel & gold bracelets (optional)	**Other Supplies** Cross Plastic zipper bags Rod pretzels or trail mix Paper Plus supplies (optional) *The Ten Plagues* Arch Book (optional)	

Active Learning Encourage the children to build houses for the people and to use the vehicles to rescue them from dangers. Tell them that in the Bible story today God sends Moses to deliver His people from a mean Pharaoh.

Use your classroom signal to let the children know it's time to clean up and gather for circle time. Sing a cleanup song (Resource Page 1).

Gathering in God's Name

What you do: Gather the children and begin with this opening. To teach about the Church Year, use the materials in the Church Year Worship Kit (see the introduction for more information).

Sing "Won't You Come and Sit with Me" (*LOSP*, p. 37; CD 18) or another song

Have the children say the Invocation and Amen with you. Before you say the Invocation. Remind the children that "Amen" is the special word they get to say at the end of prayers, hymns, and creeds, and the like.

Begin **In the name of the Father and of the Son and of the Holy Spirit. Amen.**

Offering Have a child bring the offering basket forward. Sing an offering song.

Pray **Dear God,* thank You* for loving us* and keeping us strong* when we have troubles.* Thank You for sending Jesus* to deliver us from the evil of sin.* Amen.***

*Have children echo each phrase after you.

Celebrate Birthdays, Baptism birthdays, and special occasions

2 God Speaks (20 minutes)

Story Clue

What you do: Show some action figures or pictures of familiar superheroes (e.g., Superman). Find these in books or online and show them on your tablet device. Put the action figures in your story bag, or use them with Sprout.

Say **Today I have something in my story bag that uses super powers to fight bad guys.**

Ask **What do you think it is?** Take out the action figure(s).

Say **Superheroes use their power to rescue, or deliver, people from danger and bring them to safety. It is fun to play with action figures. But they are just pretend. They aren't real, so they can't really do all the things they do on TV. But I know someone who can. Do you? Yes, God! God is real. He has all power. In today's Bible story, you will hear how He used His power to deliver His people from their troubles.**

Instead of just talking to the children, you may wish to use Sprout to introduce the story. Use the following script. Have Sprout come out holding an action figure.

Sprout: Hi, everyone! Look what I have! Ka-pow! (*Sprout flies figure through the air.*) My mom bought this for me yesterday. Isn't he great? He fights bad guys. And he rescues people from heavy cars and things like that from falling on them.

Teacher: (*Looking at figure.*) He seems pretty amazing, Sprout. It sounds like you are having fun playing with him.

Key Point

Through a series of horrific plagues, God punished the Egyptians for their sinful treatment of God's people and freed His people from bondage. Through His horrific suffering and death on the cross, Jesus takes the punishment for our sin and frees us from sin's bondage.

Sprout: Oh, yes! No one has power to fight bad guys like [Superman] does. I wish real people could do those things!

Teacher: Well, Sprout, I'm glad you are having fun pretending. But you are right—real people don't have that kind of power. But I know someone who does.

Sprout: Really? Who?

Teacher: God! God is real, and He has all power. Today, in our Bible story, we will talk about a time when God used His power to deliver His people from their troubles. Would you like to stay and listen to a true story, not a pretend one?

Sprout: Oh, yes!

Bible Story Time

What you do: Use Background B and the story figures to teach the Bible story. Use a restickable glue stick (see introduction for more information), doublestick tape, or loops of tape to attach the figures to the background. Put the figures in your Bible, and remind the children that this is a true story from God's Word. Give children turns putting the figures on the background.

Option: Find a picture of the pyramids in a book or online to show the children. Use a piece of black paper to cover the whole board for the plague of darkness.

Say   **God's people were slaves in Egypt. They had to work hard for a mean king called Pharaoh.** Show Pharaoh (7-1). **Pharaoh lived in a palace by a big river called the Nile.** Point to Nile on background and put Pharaoh in the palace. **All day long, God's people made bricks. They used the bricks to build big buildings called pyramids.** Show a picture of a pyramid if you have one. **They were tired and sad from working so hard. They prayed to God, "Dear Lord, please help us. Deliver us from this mean king."**

Ask   **Do you think God heard their prayers?**

Say   **Yes! God heard their prayers. He loved them and had a plan to save them. First, God sent Moses and Aaron to see the bad king.** Add Moses (7-2) and Aaron (7-3). **They told Pharaoh, "God says, 'Let My people go!'"**

But Pharaoh just laughed at them and said, "No, I need these people to work for me."

God did not give up. He sent Moses and Aaron back to see Pharaoh. This is what they told Pharaoh: "God said, 'If you do not let My people go, I will use My power to punish you. I will send terrible plagues to show you that I am God.'" A plague is a terrible kind of suffering that God sent to punish the Egyptian people.

Then, Moses did something to show God's power to Pharaoh. He took his shepherd's staff. Add staff (7-4) near Moses. **Then he threw the staff on the ground. Right away, it became a snake!** Replace staff with snake (7-5). **But Pharaoh still said, "No! You can't take my slaves. Now go away."**

God did not give up. He kept using His power to punish Pharaoh so Pharaoh would let God's people go. First, God used His power to turn the river into blood. Add blood (7-6) to river. **Then, He sent lots and lots of frogs. Ribbet. Ribbet. The frogs were everywhere. They hopped in the beds and out of closets. They hopped all over the food the people of Egypt ate.** Add frog (7-7).

Next, God filled the sky with teeny little bugs called gnats. The sky was black with them! Add gnat (7-8). **Then God sent buzzing flies. Buzz, buzz.** Add fly (7-9). **After that, the animals got sick. Cows and donkeys and camels started to die.** Add sick cow (7-10). **But mean Pharaoh still would not let God's people go.**

God did not give up. He kept on using His power to punish Pharaoh. He sent terrible sores called boils to cover the skin of the people. Add sores (7-11). **He made it hail so hard that the ground became white.** Add hail (7-12). **But Pharaoh still would not listen to God. He would not let God's people go!**

Then God sent bugs called locusts. Add locust (7-13). **The locusts ate every plant and piece of fruit that was left in the country. Now there was nothing left for the people to eat! Finally, God made it so dark that no one could see.** Add darkness (7-14), or cover board with black paper. **The sun didn't shine for three days.**

Ask Do you think Pharaoh changed his mind? Shake head sadly. **No, he didn't. Each time, Pharaoh said, "No, I won't let God's people go!"**

Say Through all these terrible plagues, God was at work. He was using His power to punish mean Pharaoh. He was using His power to deliver His people from trouble and bring them to a new land.

Sin causes suffering and troubles and even death. But God has power over sin and death too. He showed this when He sent Jesus to deliver us from sin and evil. When Jesus died on the cross and rose again, He won the victory over sin, death, and the devil for us. Through Jesus, God brings us to the new land of heaven.

Bible Story Review

What you do: Show Lesson Leaflet 7 and use the questions to review the story, or play If I Were Pharaoh. Provide a towel and gold bracelets for Pharaoh to wear. At the end of the game, briefly review the story.

Then hand out the leaflets, and crayons or markers. Have children draw lines to match the pictures in the sidebar with the Bible story picture. Tell them to read the story and do the dot-to-dot and other activities on the back with grown-ups at home.

Ask **Where are all the frogs coming from?** God sent them.

What does God want Moses to tell Pharaoh? Let My people go.

What other things does God do to deliver His people? Accept answers, mentioning the various plagues.

How does God deliver you? He sent Jesus to deliver us from sin and death.

Option: To play If I Were Pharaoh, have children take turns being Pharaoh. When it is their turn, give them a towel to wear as a headpiece and gold bracelets for their wrists. (You can make bracelets out of yellow paper.)

Pharaoh says, "If I were Pharaoh, you would have to [make bricks]." Have the rest of the children act out Pharaoh's orders. Help children with ideas for jobs (e.g., make cookies, make toys, build roads). Talk about how Pharaoh made God's people work so hard that they prayed to God to rescue them, and He did!

Ask **How did God use His power to deliver His people? What did Pharaoh do?**

Bible Words

What you do: Read Psalm 46:1 from your Bible, or play track 5 of the CD.

Ask Whose help did the people need? God's! Whose help do we need? God's!

Say Our Bible Words from Psalm 46:1 tell us: **"God *is* our . . . help in trouble."** **Let's learn these words now. First, listen while I name a time that we need help. Then join me in saying the Bible Words.** Be dramatic when you say your lines (e.g., look anxious, turn corners of mouth down for "sad" or look angry on "mad.") Say the refrain with the children.

Say **When we're worried and sad or need help or feel mad,**

Children: God is our . . . help in trouble.

When things aren't going right or we're scared in the night,

Children: God is our . . . help in trouble.

When we're feeling quite blue and don't know what to do,

Children: God is our . . . help in trouble.

Ask **Who is our help in times of trouble?** God! **Can you whisper it?** Do so. **Now let's say it louder.** Do so.

Option: Play the Bible Words song and have children sing along.

3 We Live (20 minutes)

Use these activities to help the children grow in their understanding of what the Bible story means for their lives. Choose the ones that work best with your class.

Growing through God's Word

What you do: Put the Pharaoh storytelling figure (7-1) in your story bag along with a cross to talk of God's rescue through Christ.

Say **Let's see what I have in my story bag.** Take out Pharaoh.

Ask **Can you tell me about him?** (Pharaoh was mean. He made God's people work hard, and he treated them badly.) **What did God do to deliver His people from their enemy?** (God used His power to send plagues to punish Pharaoh. Through them, God was at work to rescue His people.)

Say **Sometimes we aren't kind, either. Sometimes we are mean and hit our brother or sister. Sometimes we are naughty and say "no" when our moms tell us to do something. We are sinful. We cannot get away from our sin. We cannot save ourselves. We need someone to deliver us. I wonder . . . who delivers us? I have a clue in my bag.**

Ask **What do you think it is?** Accept answers; then take out cross.

Say **It's a cross. God sent Jesus to deliver us from our sins so we wouldn't be in trouble for them anymore! Jesus died on the cross and rose again to save us from our greatest enemies—sin, death, and the devil. When we do something that we shouldn't do, we can tell God that we're sorry. God loves us and will always forgive us for Jesus' sake. Someday, He will take us to heaven to live with Jesus forever. Isn't that good news? Until then, we ask God to keep us from harm and help us when we have troubles in this life.**

Growing in CHRIST.

Craft Time

What you do: Hand out Craft Page 7, stickers, and markers. Supply small plastic zipper bags for taking the game cards or puzzles (Paper Plus) home.

Have the children add stickers to the outlines of the river, cow, locust, and Jesus, and then color the frog and fly cards so each set matches. Review the plagues and how God delivered us from evil and sin through Jesus' death and resurrection. Cut the squares apart to play a memory game.

Play a game as a class with one set, or divide the children into pairs. Show them how to turn the cards facedown; then take turns flipping two cards over at a time until they find a match. They continue turning over cards until they do not find a match. Then it is their partner's turn.

Paper Plus option: Make a copy of Activity Page 7B for each child. Have the children color the page and look for the hidden crosses. Cover the pages with clear vinyl adhesive. Cut into six to eight shapes to make a puzzle.

Snack Time

What you do: Serve pretzel rods dipped in chocolate (for Moses' staff) or trail mix made with pretzels, raisins, M&Ms, and mini marshmallows. Show Poster E. Point out that Moses carried a shepherd's staff with him to lead his sheep to grass and water. Give students pretzels or trail mix.

Live It Out

Read *The Ten Plagues* Arch Book (CPH, 59-1608). Then have students create a digital book. Assign each child to draw a picture of one of the scenes of the story. Write what they say for the caption. Create a page with the Bible Words on it. Take digital pictures of their illustrations, and make them into a PowerPoint slide "book" or use your tablet to make a video.

Invite another Sunday School class to view the digital book, or arrange to show it at your Sunday School opening next week.

4 Closing (5 minutes)

Going Home

What you do: Gather materials to hand out and have your CD ready to play.

Sing "God Loves Me Dearly" (*LOSP,* p. 85; CD 10) or "Lord Jesus, Think on Me" (*LSB* 610; CD 1)

Say Today we learned that "God delivers me from sin and evil through Jesus." Let's say this together. Do so.

Pray Dear God, we're sorry when we sin. Thank You for loving us. Thank You for sending Jesus to deliver us from our sins. Amen.

Reflection

Did the children leave knowing God loves them and is their help in trouble?

God is our . . . help in trouble. Psalm 46:1

God is our . . . help in trouble. Psalm 46:1

Look for the hidden crosses.

Preparing the Lesson

The Passover

Exodus 11–12

_____
Date of Use

Key Point

Christ is our Passover Lamb, whose blood was shed for our forgiveness, life, and salvation.

Law/**Gospel**

As a sinner, I fear death. **In Christ, I look forward to eternal life; I no longer have to fear death.**

Context

Pharaoh's continued unbelief unleashes the tenth and final plague on Egypt. God Himself swoops onto the land at midnight and kills the firstborn sons of all Egypt. However, He saves those who, in faith, take hyssop and smear their doorposts in the blood of a male lamb without blemish. The Passover finally causes Pharaoh to let the Hebrews go.

Commentary

God works in mysterious ways. Rationally, we cannot fathom how the sacrificing of a year-old male lamb without blemish can turn back almighty God in His righteous anger. We cannot understand how the blood of a lamb smeared on the doorposts of a house deters death from entering Hebrew households. How can eating this slain lamb bring forth the grace of God in the place of certain death?

Only in faith. Pointing to Jesus, John the Baptizer says to us, "Behold, the Lamb of God, who takes away the sin of the world!" (John 1:29). When our Paschal Lamb drinks from the wine-drenched hyssop branch on the wooden doorposts of His cross, God marks the world as redeemed. God forever ensures that He will now pass over all who look in faith for deliverance from eternal death to His firstborn Son, slain. By Christ's coating of the cross in His holy blood, He destroys the power of death over us and delivers us into everlasting life.

It is no coincidence that Christ institutes His Holy Supper on the day "on which the Passover lamb had to be sacrificed" (Luke 22:7). On this day, Christ takes bread and wine and speaks faith-fathomable reality: "Take, eat; this is My body. . . . Drink of it, all of you, for this is My blood" (Matthew 26:26–28). When we partake of the Supper, we eat the very flesh of the new Passover Lamb. Christ puts His holy blood on the doorposts of our mouths at the altar. Thus, He passes over every reality-denying bit of us and gives us tangible proof of His mercy, for we "taste and see that the Lord is good!" (Psalm 34:8).

In His Supper, Christ causes us to put aside reason and look upon Him in faith. He gives us this faith so that we see Him in true reality, as the Lamb without blemish whose death rescues us from the sin-directed wrath of God. "For Christ, our Passover lamb, has been sacrificed" (1 Corinthians 5:7). May the God of all mercy continue to call us in faith to His altar, so that we may receive the blessings of His sacrificial death in our eating of the flesh of our Paschal Lamb, Jesus Christ.

To hear an in-depth discussion of this Bible account, visit cph.org/podcast and listen to our Seeds of Faith podcast each week.

Lesson 8

The Passover

Exodus 11–12

Connections

Bible Words
Fear not! Behold, your God will come . . . and save you. Isaiah 35:4

Faith Word
Save

Hymn
Lord Jesus, Think on Me (*LSB* 610; CD 1)

Catechism
Holy Communion

Liturgy
The Agnus Dei

Take-Home Promise
Jesus is the Lamb of God, who saves me from my sins.

1 Opening (15 minutes)

Welcome Time

What you do: Before class, set up two activity areas to provide a connection from what children know to what they will learn in the Bible lesson. In one, put out copies of Activity Page 8A, crayons or markers, corn stickers (Sticker Page), green tissue paper, glue sticks, and scissors. Make copies of Activity Page Fun (below and on CD) for parents or classroom helpers.

In the other activity area, set out paper plates, scissors, glue sticks, and seasonal decorations for making a wreath (e.g., popcorn kernels or leaves; green tissue paper and imitation holly; or spring or summer flowers).

Say Hi, [Allie]. It's good to see you here! I wonder . . . do you have a wreath or other decoration on your door? Today we'll talk about a special way God's people marked their doors.

Direct children to the tables where you have the activities. Encourage parents or caregivers to stay and do the welcome activity with their child.

Activity Page Fun Get a copy of Activity Page 8A and a corn sticker. Talk about ways we decorate our houses or doors for special times of the year.

Ask Do you like to help decorate our house for the holidays? What are some things we do for [name a holiday]? Sometimes people decorate their doors for a special holiday or season of the year. Let's decorate the wreath on this door for fall time. Color the wreath and door. Add a corn sticker to the wreath. The Bible talks about a special day of celebration called Passover. Today you will hear about the first Passover and how people marked their doors in a special way.

MATERIALS NEEDED

1 Opening	2 God Speaks	3 We Live	4 Closing
Teacher Tools Attendance chart CD	**Teacher Tools** Poster E CD	**Student Pack** Craft Page 8 Stickers	**Student Pack** Take-home materials
Student Pack Attendance & corn stickers	**Student Pack** Lesson Leaflet 8	**Other Supplies** Sprout Lamb or cross sugar cookies or pita bread & toppings Paper Plus supplies (optional)	
Other Supplies Activity Page 8A (TG) Paper plates Seasonal decorations Resource Page 1 (TG)	**Other Supplies** Sprout & travel items Activity Page 8B Paper plate, yarn & straw or ruler Robe, sandals, headpiece (optional)		

Active Learning Cut out the centers of paper plates to make a wreath shape. Give each child a plate circle along with decorating supplies to make a seasonal wreath for their doors. Talk about how we put out flags or hang things on our doors to remember special holidays.

Say **The Bible talks about a special holiday called Passover. On that day, God told His people to mark their doors in a special way so everyone inside would be safe.**

Use your classroom signal to let the children know it's time to clean up and gather for circle time. Sing a cleanup song (Resource Page 1).

Gathering in God's Name

What you do: Gather the children and begin with this opening. To teach about the Church Year, use the materials in the Church Year Worship Kit (see the introduction for more information).

Sing "Won't You Come and Sit with Me" (*LOSP*, p. 37; CD 18) or another song

Have the children say the Invocation and Amen with you. Before you say the Invocation, remind the children that "Amen" is the special word they get to say at the end of prayers, hymns, creeds, and the like.

Begin **In the name of the Father and of the Son and of the Holy Spirit. Amen.**

Offering Have a child bring the offering basket forward. Sing an offering song.

Pray **Dear Jesus,* it is good to be here* in Sunday School* to learn more about You.* Thank You for Your love.* Thank You for saving us* from our sins.* Help us to be good listeners today.* We pray in Your name.* Amen.***

*Have children echo each phrase after you.

Celebrate Birthdays, Baptism birthdays, and special occasions

2 God Speaks (20 minutes)

Story Clue

What you do: Have a conversation with Sprout. Put a few travel items, such as a toothbrush, in Sprout's backpack.

Teacher: Good morning, Sprout! It's nice to see you in Sunday School today.

Sprout: Hi, everyone! I'm super excited today!

Teacher: You look like you're happy. What's got you so full of joy?

Sprout: I'm going on a trip soon! See, I've got my backpack on, and I've got everything I need inside of it so that I can have a safe and fun time.

Teacher: Oh! Where are you going on your trip?

Sprout: I'm going to visit my grandmother. She lives far away in Canada! We have to take an airplane to get there and everything!

Teacher: That sounds like lots of fun! When you go on a trip, you have to make lots of plans so that you know where you're going, what you need to bring, and where you'll sleep and eat. In our Bible story today, God told His people to get ready to go on a trip. Let's find out what God told them to do.

Great Tip for Special Needs!

Bible Story Time

What you do: Copy Activity Page 8B. Color the face, and glue on yarn for hair. Attach it to a paper plate, and tape a straw or ruler to it to use it as a puppet. *Option:* Put on a robe, headpiece, and sandals. Tell the story as though you were Moses, or invite someone else to do so. You will also need Poster E.

If you have children with hearing impairments, enunciate clearly and make sure they can see your face.

Say **Boys and girls, this story is a true story from God's book, the Bible.** Show Bible. **It is about the amazing way God rescued His people in the middle of the night and brought them out of Egypt. It is the story of Passover. Today let's pretend that Moses is here to tell us about that night.**

Hold up the puppet face of Moses or put on the props and tell the story in a dramatic way as though you were Moses.

Say **Hi, boys and girls. My name is Moses. Do you remember me? When I was a baby, the princess of Egypt found me floating in a basket on the river. She loved me right away and made me her own son. When I grew up, I was a shepherd. One day, God talked to me from a burning bush! He told me He had a special job for me to do.**

You see, God's people were slaves in Egypt. Day and night, they worked hard for Pharaoh, the mean ruler of Egypt. God wanted to set His people free and take them to a new land. So, He sent my brother and me to Egypt to tell Pharaoh to let God's people go. But did Pharaoh listen? No! He did not obey God.

So God used His power against Pharaoh. He sent many bad troubles called plagues to Egypt. But Pharaoh still said no. Then God told me, "I will bring one more terrible plague on Egypt. After that, Pharaoh will let My people go."

I told God's people, "Get ready. Tonight God is going to pass over Egypt. During the night, the first son in every house in Egypt will die. To save the sons in your family, He wants you to put blood from a lamb around your doors. When God sees the blood of the lamb, He will pass over your house. The lamb's blood will save you from death."

Look, here's a picture of a father and son doing what God said to do. Show Poster E.

Ask **Do they look scared?** Accept answers.

Say **No. Even though this was a scary thing, we knew God loved us and would keep us safe. After that, we had to get ready for a long trip. We made special food.** Point to family in house making food. **Then we ate a special dinner and put our traveling clothes on. We packed our things and got the animals ready to go.**

God said this last terrible plague would be the Lord's Passover. That night, God passed over Egypt. In every house where there was no blood over the door, the firstborn son in the family died. But the blood of the lamb over our doors kept us safe from death.

Then Pharaoh was sorry that he had not listened to God. He told me, "Take God's people and leave right away." So, we left Egypt as fast as we could. We were excited! We were going to the new land God

Key Point

Christ is our Passover Lamb, whose blood was shed for our forgiveness, life, and salvation.

promised to give us. Put down puppet, or take off costume.

Say **God loved His people and had a plan to save them. He told them to put blood over their doors so those inside would not die. Then Moses led God's people to a new land. God loves us too. He sent Jesus to die on the cross for us. The Bible calls Jesus the Lamb of God because Jesus shed His blood on the cross to save us from sin. Because of Jesus, God gives us a new home in heaven.**

Bible Story Review

What you do: Show Poster E. Use the questions to review the story. This will help you assess what they understand. Then hand out the leaflets and crayons.

Option: Do the action rhyme "The Passover" from *Wiggle & Wonder* (CPH, 22-3130). Movement activities support learning by engaging the brain and helping children process what they have heard.

Ask **What is the man putting around his door?** Blood from a lamb

What are the people inside the house doing? Preparing a special supper

What will God do when He sees the blood around the door? He will pass over the house; those inside will not be hurt.

Who shed His blood on the cross to save you? Jesus

Hand out copies of Lesson Leaflet 8. Have the children circle the correct picture in the sidebar and color the stained glass window on the back.

Bible Words

What you do: Have your Bible open to read the verse from Isaiah 35:4.

Ask **How do you think God's people felt when Moses told them what would happen?** Accept answers.

Say **Sometimes we are afraid. Sometimes we wonder what will happen. But God gives us a special promise in His Word. He tells, "Fear not! Behold, your God will come . . . and save you." Let's use our hands and feet as we say these Bible Words together.**

Say **Fear not!**   Hold up hands up as if saying no.
Behold, your God Point up.
will come . . .   Walk in place.
and save you.   Make a cross with fingers.

Great Idea!

Liturgy Link

The words *Agnus Dei* are Latin for "Lamb of God." We sing or say the Agnus Dei in the Lutheran liturgy before Holy Communion. Talk about the lamb in the stained glass window on the leaflet. Ask the children to tell you what this image means to them.

3 We Live (20 minutes)

Use these activities to help the children grow in their understanding of what the Bible story means for their lives. Choose the ones that work best with your class.

Growing through God's Word

What you do: Use Sprout puppet again.

Teacher: Well, Sprout, have you heard that story before? It's a true story, you know.

Sprout: No. I've never heard that story before. God sure must have loved His people a lot to save them from the Egyptians and from that bad guy, Pharaoh. He got them all ready for the big trip too, didn't He?

Teacher: Yes, Sprout. God had a special plan to save His people. Did you know that God has a special plan to save us too—you and me and all of these boys and girls here today?

Sprout: REALLY? What kind of plan?

Teacher: Well, God's Word says that only people who are perfect can go to heaven, but I'm not perfect and neither are you. Sometimes I say or do wrong things. You do too.

Sprout: Yeah. I'm not always kind to my cousin Lily. Last week, I was so mad at her that I threw her doll on the floor. And sometimes, when we play hide-and-seek, I peek. That's cheating.

Teacher: Right. We all do things we shouldn't do. That's called sin. God doesn't like sin. It brings trouble and pain and sadness and sickness and even death. But God loves us and wants us to live in heaven with Him someday. That's why God made a special plan to get rid of our sin. He sent Jesus to take the punishment for our sins by dying on the cross.

Sprout: Jesus didn't stay dead though! He came back to life, right?

Teacher: That's right. Jesus came back to life again. Everyone who believes that Jesus died and rose again will live forever in heaven. It's God's special plan.

Sprout: That's so great! I feel happy when I think about how much God loves me!

Teacher: Me too, Sprout.

Craft Time

What you do: Hand out Craft Page 8 and the stickers.

Have the children cut off the strip with the tent puppets and color the figures on both sides. On side 1, have the children color the blood around the door and add stickers of the food that was eaten at Passover. Fold the page to create a story background that can stand up. Use it with the puppet to retell the story.

The other side is a story background to use with the modern-day child puppet. Children will finish coloring it and add stickers of a Communion chalice, plate of wafers, and an altar cross. Talk about how Jesus is the Lamb of God who takes away the sin of the world.

Paper Plus option: God's people painted blood around their doors so those inside would not be hurt. Copy Activity Page 8C for each child. Children can decorate and cut it out it to make a doorknob hanger to remind them of God's love in Jesus.

Say **In church, we hear how God saved us by sending Jesus to pay for our sins. God tells us He forgives us and gives us special food to eat. We celebrate God's love by worshiping Him.**

Snack Time

What you do: Serve lamb- or cross-shaped sugar cookies, or unleavened bread or pitas spread with cream cheese or jelly.

As children eat their snack, discuss special times in our lives—Thanksgiving, Christmas, birthdays—and how we celebrate them with special meals. Then talk about the special meal God's people ate before they left on their trip.

Live It Out

If you made doorknob hangers, encourage the children to put their doorknob hanger on the door of a neighbor or friend who needs to hear about God's love.

4 Closing (5 minutes)

Going Home

What you do: Give them scarves or tambourines to wave, and have a praise parade around the room. Have take-home items ready to hand out.

Sing "Jesus Came from Heaven" (*LOSP*, p. 92:1) or "Lord Jesus, Think on Me" (*LSB* 610; CD 1)

Say **Long ago, God saved His people from death through the blood of a lamb on their doors. God saved us too. He sent Jesus to die on the cross and come back to life.**

Let's say, "Jesus is the Lamb of God, who saves me from my sin" together. Do so.

Pray **Dear Jesus, thank You for saving me from my sins by dying on the cross for me and rising again. Amen.**

Reflection

Were the children involved in today's activities? Which ones held their attention? Which ones were too difficult? How can you adjust future lessons with this in mind?

Color and cut out. Glue the face to a paper plate, and attach the plate to a ruler to make a storytelling puppet.

God is our
. . . help
in trouble.

Psalm 46:1

Preparing the Lesson

Crossing the Red Sea

Exodus 13:17–15:21

Date of Use

Key Point

As God saved the Hebrews through the water of the Red Sea, He saves us through the washing of water in Holy Baptism, conquering Satan, our greatest enemy.

Law/**Gospel**

The waves of this sinful world surge around me and drain me of life. **The waters of Holy Baptism wash me clean of sin and grant me life eternal.**

Context

Pharaoh lets the Hebrews go, but he soon regrets having done so. Pharaoh unleashes his unholy host upon the hapless Hebrews and quickly overtakes them. God fights for His people as a pillar of cloud and fire. In the hand of Moses, God's staff parts the Red Sea, thereby giving dry ground so the children of Israel might cross. Afterward, God topples the watery walls of the sea and destroys the very army bent on the destruction of His people.

Commentary

Hopeless! Perhaps we feel hopeless at times. We see no way out of our situations. Our sins, this world, even the devil and his minions envelop our entire view and obscure all hope.

The Israelites feel hopeless. All the wanting in the world cannot give them the power to defeat the mighty armies seeking to subjugate them again. Likewise, wave after wave of watery death stands before them. Fearing the circumstances, they respond naturally by grumbling: "Is it because there are no graves in Egypt that you have taken us away to die in the wilderness?" (Exodus 14:11). Whereas our eyes see only death by sword or water, God speaks salvation: "Fear not, stand firm, and see the salvation of the LORD" (Exodus 14:13). Thus, the water parts, providing a pathway to paradise for God's people.

This salvation for the children of Israel in the crossing of the Red Sea foreshadows the watery deliverance of the new Israel. Thus, "all were baptized into Moses in the cloud and in the sea" (1 Corinthians 10:2). Likewise, in the Red Sea of Christ's crucifixion, Christ's blood purges the demonic death grip that the devil has on God's creation. On Calvary, Christ takes the worst that this world can dish out and bears the marks of our sinful complaints on His beaten and bloodied body.

Thus, Christ restores hope for us. God gives this hope to us in His same watery way. In our Baptism, we "stand firm, and see the salvation of the LORD." God tinges crimson our Red Sea baptismal fonts by the blood of His Son. In our consecrated baptismal waters, God washes away our sinful griping and the pursuing Egyptian demons.

From font to funeral, God continually fills us with His hope because He drenched us by His "washing of regeneration and renewal of the Holy Spirit" (Titus 3:5). We are never hopeless because God promises to fight for us. "Let us draw near . . . with our hearts sprinkled clean from an evil conscience and our bodies washed with pure water. Let us hold fast the confession of our hope without wavering, for He who promised is faithful" (Hebrews 10:22–23)

To hear an in-depth discussion of this Bible account, visit cph.org/podcast and listen to our Seeds of Faith podcast each week.

Lesson 9

Crossing the Red Sea

Exodus 13:17–15:21

Connections

Bible Words
Fear not, stand firm, and see the salvation of the Lord. Exodus 14:13 (CD 4)

Faith Word
Rescue

Hymn
O Sing to the Lord (*LSB* 808; CD 2)

Catechism
Holy Baptism

Liturgy
Holy Baptism

Take-Home Promise
God saves me.

 Opening (15 minutes)

Welcome Time

What you do: Before class, set up two activity areas. In one, put out copies of Activity Page 9, Jesus stickers, and crayons or markers. Make copies of Activity Page Fun (below and on CD) for parents or classroom helpers.

In the other activity area, set out a dishpan partially filled with water, toy people, and objects that sink and float. To catch spills, set the items on a large towel.

Say   Hi, [Max]. I am glad to see you today. I wonder . . . have you ever gone over a river? How did you do it? Did you walk? Did you fly? Did you drive on a bridge? Today you'll hear how God's people crossed a big river.

Direct children to the tables where you have the activities. Encourage parents or caregivers to stay and do the welcome activity with their child.

Activity Page Fun Get a copy of Activity Page 9 and a sticker. Talk about the people who need help in the house and cars. Have your child draw lines to match the people in danger to those who can rescue them.

Say   Draw lines to match someone in danger with the rescue worker who can help. Today you'll hear how God loved His people and saved them from their enemy. Point to the cross made by the intersecting lines. **God loves you too. He sent Jesus to save you from sin.** Give your child a Jesus sticker to put on the cross as a reminder of God's rescue.

MATERIALS NEEDED

1 Opening	2 God Speaks	3 We Live	4 Closing
Teacher Tools Attendance chart CD	**Teacher Tools** CD	**Student Pack** Craft Page 9 Sticker	**Teacher Tools** CD
Student Pack Attendance sticker & Jesus sticker	**Student Pack** Lesson Leaflet 9	**Other Supplies** Yarn	**Student Pack** Take-home materials
Other Supplies Activity Page 9 (TG) Tub of water Floating objects & toy people Resource Page 1 (TG) Scarves or rhythm instruments	**Other Supplies** Sprout *Moses' Dry Feet* Arch Book (optional)	Art supplies Blue gelatin & jelly beans Storybooks or pictures of fears (optional) Paper Plus supplies (optional)	

Active Learning Set out a dishpan partially filled with water, some toy people, and an assortment of objects to float in the water.

Ask **Which ones float? Which ones sink?** Give children toy people. **How can these little people get across the water to the other side?**

Say **Today you will hear how God saved His people from their enemy by helping them get across a lot of water.**

Use your classroom signal to let the children know it's time to clean up and gather for circle time. Sing a cleanup song (Resource Page 1).

Gathering in God's Name

What you do: Use this opening format each week so that children become familiar with it. To teach about the Church Year, use the materials in the Church Year Worship Kit (see the introduction for more information).

In Baptism, we, like the Israelites, passed through water and were saved. Our old Adam drowned, and God raised a new person to life. We respond with praise and thanks just as the Israelites did. Young children will not understand this analogy, but they can grasp that water washes them and rejoice in being God's children. Give them chiffon scarves, jingle bells threaded on chenille wires then twisted closed, or rhythm instruments to use as they sing the opening song.

Sing "Won't You Come and Sit with Me" (*LOSP*, p. 11; CD 18) or another song

Have the children say the Invocation and Amen with you. Tell them "Amen" is the special word they get to say at the end of prayers, hymns, and the like.

Begin **In the name of the Father and of the Son and of the Holy Spirit. Amen.**

Offering Have a child bring the offering basket forward. Sing an offering song.

Pray **Dear God,* thank You* for washing away my sin* and making me Your child* in Baptism.* Thank You* for always taking care of me.* Amen.***

*Have children echo each phrase after you.

Celebrate Birthdays, Baptism birthdays, and special occasions

2 God Speaks (20 minutes)

Story Clue

What you do: Use Sprout to provide a connection from experiences the children have to what they will learn in the Bible lesson.

Teacher: Hi, Sprout! I'm glad you made it to Sunday School today. How are you?

Sprout: Hi, Teacher. Hi, kids. I'm g-r-e-a-t today! But yesterday, I had a big scare. My mom took Lily and me to a big park. There were slides to go down and bridges to run across and a jungle gym with bars to cross and places to peek through.

Teacher: It sounds like you and Lily were having a good time. What happened to scare you?

Sprout: Well, we were playing tag. Lily was it. She chased me over the bridges and followed me down the slides. Then, I came to those bars that you have to hang on to get across. I'm not too good at those, but I had to get away from Lily! I climbed up the ladder and grabbed the first bar. I swung to the next one. But then my arms got tired. I didn't want Lily to catch me, so I couldn't go back. But I couldn't go forward either. My arms started to hurt from trying to hold on! I was sure I would fall. I was so scared!

Teacher: Oh, no, Sprout. What did you do?

Sprout: I called out, "Help!" My mom heard me and came running to help.

Teacher: So, your mom came to the rescue! I'm glad!

Sprout: Yup! So am I! She put her arms around me so I could hang on. With my mom's help, I made it all the way to the other side! And Lily didn't catch me!

Teacher: Your mom loves you a lot, Sprout. She saved you from getting hurt. In our Bible story today, God's people, the Israelites, were being chased by Pharaoh. They were scared too. But God was watching over them. He saved them from danger in a special way. Let's listen and find out how!

Bible Story Time

What you do: Tell the story as a chalk talk using the following script. *Option:* Use the Arch Book *Moses' Dry Feet* (CPH, 59-1518) to tell the story.

Say **God's people, the Israelites, were in a big hurry. They worked hard every day for bad king Pharaoh. God saw their hurt and heard their prayers. He sent many troubles called plagues on Egypt. Finally, Pharaoh said they could leave.**

Moses told the people, "Hurry, hurry! Go pack your clothes and food." Draw suitcase. **"It is time to go. You don't have to work as slaves anymore. God told me to take you to a new land where you will be safe." So, the people gathered their animals and belongings. They asked God to protect them. Then, they hurried out of Egypt.**

It was a long trip to the new land. The people walked and walked. Walk in place. **But God was with them. During the day, God led the way in a pillar of cloud. At night, He led them with a pillar of fire and gave them light to see.** Draw a pillar to show cloud/fire.

Finally, Moses and the people came to some water called the Red Sea. They were hungry and tired, so they decided to stay there for the night. Soon, the dads were setting up tents for camp. Draw tent. **Moms made supper, and little children played by the edge of the water. Suddenly, the people heard a rumbling noise faraway.**

Oh no! A big army was coming toward them. Bad king Pharaoh had changed his mind. He was bringing his chariots and horses and soldiers to take the people back to Egypt. Draw stick soldiers. **God's people were afraid! How could they get away from mean Pharaoh?**

Right in front of them was a huge sea! Draw waves. **There was too much water to go around the sea. There was no bridge for them to go over the sea. They did not have boats to sail across the sea. "What will happen to us?" the people cried.**

Moses knew God would help them. He told the people, "Don't be afraid. God promised to be with us. He will fight for us today and keep us safe. He will rescue us from our enemies." Then, God's cloud moved so it was between the people and Pharaoh's army. Now the soldiers couldn't see what was happening. Draw cloud or point to cloud you already drew.

God told Moses, "Stretch out your walking stick over the water." When Moses did this, something amazing happened. A big wind began to blow. It made a dry path with two big walls of water on either side. Erase middle of wavy lines to represent dry path. **Moses and God's people walked on this dry path between the walls of water to the other side.**

Pharaoh's army tried to follow them along the path, but God made the wheels fall off their chariots. Finally, when Moses and the people were safe on the other side, God told Moses, "Hold your walking stick over the sea again." Moses did this, and God made the walls of water splash together again. Close up the wavy lines again. **The water covered the horses and chariots and soldiers. Not one of them got away.**

That's how God rescued His people from Pharaoh and his armies! The people were so happy. They danced and sang and played musical instruments to praise God for saving them. Draw smiley face.

God loves us too. He rescued us from our enemies of sin, death, and the devil. He did this by sending Jesus to be our Savior. Draw cross. **He saves us through the water of Holy Baptism by washing away our sins and making us His children. When we are worried or afraid, we can remember that we belong to Him. He loves us and will take care of us. Someday, He will take us to a new home in heaven.**

Bible Story Review

What you do: Hand out Lesson Leaflet 9 and crayons or markers. Show the picture, and use the questions to review the story. Then have the children color and look for the sidebar figures in the Bible art. The activity on the back can be done in class or at home.

Option: Have the children act out this dramatic Bible rescue story. When you talk about how the people sang and danced to praise God for saving them, play "O Sing to the Lord" (*LSB* 808; CD 2) on your CD. Give children scarves, jingle bells, or rhythm instruments to use as they sing and have a praise parade.

Ask **How did God's people get across the water?** God parted the water so they could walk across on dry land.

What is Moses doing now? He is holding out his staff so the waters come back together again.

How did God save His people? He rescued them from their enemies.

How does God save you? He sent Jesus to save us from our sins.

Bible Words

What you do: Read the Bible Words from the Bible. Play them on the CD.

Say **God's people were scared! They needed help. How did God save them?** Let children tell. **Sometimes we're scared too. We need help. God tells us in the Bible, "Don't be afraid." He says** (read from Bible), **"Fear not, stand firm, and see the salvation of the Lord."** Listen to the Bible Words on the CD, or say them with the children.

Fear not,	Cross hands in front as if saying no.
stand firm,	Stomp left foot; stomp right foot; stand still.
and see the salvation	Cup hand over eyes.
of the Lord.	Make cross with fingers.

③ We Live (20 minutes)

Use these activities to help the children grow in their understanding of what the Bible story means for their lives. Choose the ones that work best with your class.

Growing through God's Word

What you do: No special supplies are needed. If you wish, show pictures in storybooks or on your tablet device that depict common fears the children may have.

Say God's people were being chased by enemies. They were afraid.

Ask Have any of you ever been afraid? What makes you afraid? Let children talk about their fears. If they don't volunteer any, tell of a time you were afraid.

What can we do when we are afraid? Accept responses.

Say One thing we can do is pray. We can talk to God about what we are afraid of and ask Him to make us brave.

We can remember that God used His mighty power to rescue His people. God used His mighty power to save us from our enemies of sin, death, and the devil. He did this by sending Jesus to be our Savior.

God saved His people, bringing them safely through the water of the Red Sea. God saves us through the waters of Baptism by washing away our sins and making us His children.

Today you'll make a picture that you can hang in your room. It will help remind you that God loves you so much that He sent Jesus to be your Savior. You belong to Him. Jesus promises in His Word that He will be with you always, even in the scary times. Someday, He will take us to a new home in heaven.

Craft Time

What you do: You will need Craft Page 9, the sticker of Jesus, yarn, a hole punch, glue sticks, and art supplies to personalize crosses.

First, talk about the pictures that show fears. Then cut out the cross. Have the children glue the cutout corner pictures to the cross. Talk about how Jesus is with us when we are afraid.

Give the children markers, snippets of colored paper or sandpaper, textured yarn, and other art supplies to decorate the blank side of the cross. They can put the sticker of Jesus on the middle of the cross. Punch a hole in the top, and thread yarn through it so the children can hang the cross at home.

Ask What shape is left when we cut the pictures off? (A cross) Whom does the cross remind us of? Jesus!

Say When we're scared, we can talk to God. He will always listen to our prayers and help us in a way that is best. Let's glue the pictures onto the cross to remind us that God is with us and will take care of us. He used His mighty power to save us from our sins by sending Jesus to die on the cross for us. We don't have to be afraid.

Paper Plus option: When God saved the Israelites, they sang and danced and played musical instruments to praise God for His love. Help the children make

Key Point

As God saved the Hebrews through the water of the Red Sea, He saves us through the washing of water in Holy Baptism, conquering Satan, our greatest enemy.

tambourines by punching several holes around the edge of a paper plate. Put a piece of chenille wire (pipe cleaner) through each hole. Thread a jingle bell onto each wire; then twist the wire closed. Give the children decorating supplies and markers to personalize their tambourine.

Snack Time

What you do: Make a pan of blue finger gelatin. Cut into rectangles and give each student one. Talk about how it reminds us of water. Cut each piece in half. Give the children some jelly beans or jelly babies to walk across the path as you retell the story. Talk about how the blue also makes you think of the water of Baptism. Talk about this very special day. *Option:* Before class, take pictures that show Baptisms or baptismal mementos on your tablet device or smartphone (e.g., baptismal font, gown, candle, pictures of families at a Baptism). Show these as you talk about Baptism.

Live It Out

Have the children learn the hymn "O Sing to the Lord" (*LSB* 808; CD 2). Ask your pastor if they can sing it in church some Sunday. Give them rhythm instruments and praise wavers to "play" as they sing.

 **4 Closing** (5 minutes)

Going Home

What you do: Gather take-home materials to hand out. Ask children to name specific worries or fears they have to include in your prayer. Pray for children by name, or help those who wish to pray to offer a simple prayer for themselves or a friend.

Sing "O Sing to the Lord" (*LSB* 808; CD 2) or "I Was Baptized" (*LOSP*, p. 97)

Say **Our God is so great! He saved His people from their enemies by making a safe path through the water. God saved us too! He sent Jesus to die on the cross for us. He washes away our sin through Holy Baptism.**

Let's say "God saves me" together. Do so.

Pray **Dear God, You saved Your people from their enemies. Thank You for sending Jesus to save us from our enemies—sin, death, and the devil. When we are afraid of** [name a worry or fear], **help us remember that You love us and are with us. For Jesus' sake, we pray. Amen.**

Reflection

Today's lesson gives children the opportunity to learn that God is bigger than their fears. What activities helped them express confidence in God's love and care for them? How can you continue to emphasize God's saving love in Jesus in the weeks to come?

Draw a line from those who need help to something that will rescue them.

Preparing the Lesson

God Provides Manna, Water, and Quail

Exodus 16–17

Date of Use

Key Point

In Christ, God feeds us with the manna of His Word and the water of His forgiveness, satisfying our eternal hunger and quenching our spiritual thirst.

Law/**Gospel**

My attempts to satisfy myself with all good things cannot fill the void that sin creates in my life. **Christ—by His suffering, death, and resurrection—fills me to overflowing with His life-giving grace and mercy.**

Context

Escaping the clutches of drowned Pharaoh, the Israelites find themselves wandering in the desert without food and water. Humankind, in sinful unbelief, soon begins to grumble about the lack of amenities. Yet, God provides for His people. God "commanded the skies above and opened the doors of heaven, and He rained down on them manna to eat and gave them the grain of heaven" (Psalm 78:23–24). Moreover, God Himself stands before Moses on the rock. As Moses strikes, water gushes forth to quench Israel's thirst.

Commentary

Any number of life's maladies can overwhelm us and leave us hanging out to dry in our deserts of doubt. A job loss or a serious illness can leave us fretting over the basic things of this world, even food and drink.

The Israelites worry too, because they hunger. Sand seemingly scattered everywhere disheartens this group of depressed desert drifters. A Promised Land flowing with milk and honey seems worlds away to ravenous stomachs and dry, chapped lips. This anxious distrust in the Father festers into sinful unbelief.

"Which one of you, if his son asks him for bread, will give him a stone?" (Matthew 7:9). If we, who are evil, know how to give good gifts to our children, how much more will our Father in heaven give good gifts! God always acts against our unbelief. He loves us enough to provide for us. Thus, God rains bread from heaven for His people and creates water from a rock simply by the striking of a staff.

Likewise, our Father gives us the true bread from heaven, Jesus Christ. God provides us His Son so that we "shall not live by bread alone, but by every word that comes from the mouth of God" (Matthew 4:4). In His Word, we partake of the same spiritual rock from which the Israelites drank, for "the Rock was Christ" (1 Corinthians 10:4).

Regardless of the extent of our desert surroundings, we have no worries because God fills us with Christ through His Word! On account of the Lord's atoning sacrifice, His Word speaks absolution. In His Word, forgiveness rains down as manna. Forgiveness pours forth as soothing waters from our Rock's stricken side. This water, infused with grace, quenches our thirsting throats and reinvigorates worry-worn souls. Satiated by the Word, let us with carefree hearts "make a joyful noise to the rock of our salvation!" (Psalm 95:1).

To hear an in-depth discussion of this Bible account, visit cph.org/podcast and listen to our Seeds of Faith podcast each week.

Preparing the Lesson © 2007, 2015 Concordia Publishing House. Scripture: ESV®.

Lesson 10

God Provides Manna, Water, and Quail

Exodus 16–17

Connections

Bible Words
The LORD will provide.
Genesis 22:14

Faith Words
Provide
Satisfied

Hymn
O Sing to the Lord (*LSB* 808; CD 2)

Catechism
Apostles' Creed: First Article

Take-Home Promise
God provides for me.

(1) Opening (15 minutes)

Welcome Time

What you do: Before class, set up two activity areas. In one, put out copies of Activity Page 10A and crayons or markers. Make copies of Activity Page Fun (below and on CD) for parents or classroom helpers.

In the other activity area, set out 11 × 17-inch paper, paper plates, glue sticks, and crayons or markers. *Option:* Set out food magazines and scissors or play dough. Play "The First Article" (CD 20) as the children work.

Say   Hi, [Ava]. I like your shoes. I wonder . . . who gave them to you? Today you'll hear how God gives us what we need. He provides for us.

Direct children to the tables where you have the activities. Encourage parents or caregivers to stay and do the welcome activity with their child.

Activity Page Fun Get a copy of Activity Page 10A. Have your child tell you about the picture, then color the basket and fruit. Cut the food apart and let your child choose which foods to put in the basket, or ask your child to draw lines to connect the food to the basket.

Say   Pretend you are going on a picnic. What is your favorite food? Which of these foods would you pack in the basket to take with you? Today you'll hear about a time God's people, the Israelites, were hungry and wanted something good to eat. Listen and find out what they ate.

© 2015 Concordia Publishing House. Reproduced by permission. Available on the Teacher CD.

MATERIALS NEEDED

1 Opening	2 God Speaks	3 We Live	4 Closing
Teacher Tools Attendance chart CD	**Teacher Tools** Background A Poster F	**Student Pack** Craft Page 10 Stickers	**Teacher Tools** CD
Student Pack Attendance sticker	**Student Pack** Lesson Leaflet 10	**Other Supplies** Sprout Nilla wafers & water Paper Plus supplies (optional)	**Student Pack** Take-home materials
Other Supplies Activity Page 10A (TG) Paper plates Magazine pictures or play dough (optional) Resource Page 1 (TG)	**Other Supplies** Grocery sack & groceries Beanbag *Moses and the Long Walk* Arch Book (optional)		

Active Learning Give each child a sheet of paper and a paper plate to make a place mat with a table setting. Have children glue the plate to the middle of the paper, then draw a napkin and silverware beside the plate. Children can decorate their place mat and then draw or glue pictures of what they like to eat to their plate, or use play dough to make food for their plate. Allowing children to personalize their place mats gives them the opportunity to be creative and experience ownership, which in turn, helps build insights.

Say **God provides everything we need. He gives us food and a place to sleep, clothes to wear and people who love us. God also gives us Jesus, who came to be our Savior. Jesus loves us so much!**

Use your classroom signal to let the children know it's time to clean up and gather for circle time. Sing a cleanup song (Resource Page 1).

Gathering in God's Name

What you do: Use this opening format each week so that children become familiar with it. To teach about the Church Year, use the materials in the Church Year Worship Kit (see the introduction for more information).

Sing "Won't You Come and Sit with Me" (*LOSP*, p. 11; CD 18) or another song

Have the children say the Invocation and Amen with you. Tell them "Amen" is the special word they get to say at the end of prayers, hymns, and the like.

Begin **In the name of the Father and of the Son and of the Holy Spirit. Amen.**

Offering Have a child bring the offering basket forward. Sing an offering song.

Pray **Dear God, thank You for food to fill our tummies and houses to keep us warm. Thank You for giving us everything we need. Thank You, most of all, for Jesus and for forgiving our sins. Amen.**

Celebrate Birthdays, Baptism birthdays, and special occasions

2 God Speaks (20 minutes)

Story Clue

What you do: Put food items in a grocery bag. Include a cake mix and can of frosting, along with some dinner items (a can of corn, a box of Jell-O, apple, etc.). *Option:* Find pictures of the food items online or in a book to show children.

Say **Boys and girls, what are some things you do for holidays like Christmas or the Fourth of July or special days like birthdays?** Accept answers. **I have something in my bag that my family likes to do when we celebrate special days. What do you think I brought?** Allow guesses; then take out the birthday items. **I have a box of cake mix.**

Ask **Do you like cake? Who likes chocolate cake best? Who likes white cake?** Take out frosting. **What can I do with this? What is the special day that we often eat cake or cupcakes? What other things might we eat?** Continue with remaining foods.

Say **All this food makes me hungry just looking at it! It will make a good dinner!**

Ask **Where do you think I got this food?** Allow suggestions.

Say You are right. I bought this food at the grocery store. God sends sun and rain to make food grow. The farmers take the food to the store. The grocery store sells the food to us. Then, we eat the food so we aren't hungry! In today's Bible story, God's people are hungry. They don't have any food to eat. There are no grocery stores nearby to buy the food. But God provides for them. That means He gives them what they need. Let's listen and find out what God does!

Bible Story Time

What you do: Use Poster F and Background A. Cut apart the figures and place them in your Bible. Remind children that this is a true story from God's Word. Use loops of tape or a restickable glue stick to attach the figures to the background.

Say A desert is a very hot place. Water is hard to find, so not many plants or animals live in the desert. In today's Bible story, Moses was leading God's people through a big desert. Add people (10-5) to the background. **At night, they camped in tents under the stars.** Add tent (10-1). **But the people were not happy.** Shake head no. **They were hot, and they were hungry. The food they brought from Egypt was gone. There were no plants or animals to eat. There were no grocery stores or restaurants to buy food.**

"We have nothing to eat!" they complained to Moses. "You brought us out here where it is hot and sandy. You said you were taking us to a better place to live. But now we have nothing to eat! We should have stayed in Egypt. We weren't hungry there."

Moses told God about their grumbling. God said, "I will provide for My people. At night, I will send birds they can eat. In the morning, I will send bread." That night, God kept His promise. Suddenly, lots and lots of birds called quail flew to the place where the people were camping. Add bird (10-3). **God's people caught the birds and cooked them for supper. Now their tummies were full again. For breakfast, God covered the ground with something that looked like snow. It was special bread that tasted like honey. The people called it manna.** Add manna (10-2).

Soon, God's people packed up their tents and walked again. Remove tent. **God kept sending birds and manna for them to eat.** Point to birds and manna. **But now they had no water. They were hot, and they were thirsty! So, they grumbled again, "Moses, why did you take us out of Egypt? We had plenty of water there. There is nothing to drink here! We are dying of thirst!"**

God heard their grumbling. He knew His people needed something to drink. He told Moses, "Hit that rock with your stick." Moses hit the rock, and water came gushing out. Add water (10-4). **The people drank water from the rock. How good it tasted! Now they weren't thirsty anymore.**

God provided for His people. He gave them a leader to show them the way. He gave them tent homes to live in. He gave them food to eat. He gave them water to drink. They grumbled and complained, but God forgave them.

God provides for us too. He gives us people to care for us. He gives us homes to live in. He gives us food to eat. He gives us water and other good things to drink. Still we grumble and complain. We sin. But God forgives us for the sake of Jesus, who paid for our sin on the cross.

Key Point

In Christ, God feeds us with the manna of His Word and the water of His forgiveness, satisfying our eternal hunger and quenching our spiritual thirst.

Bible Story Review

What you do: Hand out Lesson Leaflet 10 and crayons. Review the story with the questions; then describe the objects in the sidebar. Have the children count how many of each they can find in the Bible art and color the pictures. Answers may vary. Encourage the children to read the story and do the activity on the back with a grown-up at home.

Option: Review the story using the Arch Book *Moses and the Long Walk* (CPH, 59-1607).

Ask **What are the people doing?** Collecting manna

Where did the food come from? God sent it.

What does God tell Moses to do when the people are thirsty? Strike a rock. When Moses does, water comes out.

How does God provide for you? Accept answers.

Sing "God Is So Good" (*LOSP*, p. 57; CD 8).

Have the children name things God gives them and sing stanzas using those suggestions (e.g., God gives me [pizza], God gives me [pizza], God gives me [pizza]. He's so good to me). End with "God gives me Jesus, God gives me Jesus, God gives me Jesus. He's so good to me."

Bible Words

What you do: You will need your Bible to read Genesis 22:14, "The Lord will provide."

Say **Our Bible Words for today are from Genesis 22:14.** Show children where the words come from in the Bible. **Listen while I read them: The Lord will provide.**

Ask **How does God provide for us?** Accept answers, such as He gives us food and things to drink. **What other ways does God provide for us?** Help children see that God gives us all good things: parents, teachers, clothes, friends, a home, our church where we learn about Him, and so on.

Say **Let's learn our words. I will toss a beanbag to one of you. When you get the beanbag, say, "The Lord will provide," then toss it to a friend who hasn't had it yet. We'll do this till everyone has a turn to say the Bible Words.**

Teacher Tip

All young children need to use their large muscles. Providing a planned stretch activity between sit-down times is especially beneficial for those with attention problems. See Resource Page 1.

3 We Live (20 minutes)

Use these activities to help the children grow in their understanding of what the Bible story means for their lives. Choose the ones that work best with your class.

Growing through God's Word

What you do: Have Sprout appear, grumbling to himself.

Teacher: Hi, Sprout. You don't sound so happy today. What's wrong?

Sprout: Broccoli! That's what's wrong. Lily invited me to her house for supper tonight, and my mom said I could go. Then Lily told me her mom is cooking chicken and mashed potatoes and *broccoli*!

Teacher: Hmm, it sounds like you don't like broccoli.

Sprout: Yuck! It's nasty. But my mom said I have to be a good guest and try a few bites. I wish I didn't have to go to Lily's now.

Teacher: Oh, Sprout, your grumbling reminds me of God's people in our Bible story today!

Sprout: What do you mean? I'm not grumbling because I have nothing to eat! I . . .

Teacher: (*Interrupting*) No, you're grumbling because you *have* got good food to eat, but you still aren't satisfied with it!

Sprout: What does that mean—satisfied?

Teacher: It means God has given you good food, but you want something else. You aren't happy and content with what He gives you. You don't like it.

Sprout: Oh. (*Hanging head*) I guess grumbling and not being thankful for what God gives us is a sin, isn't it, Teacher?

Teacher: Yes, it is, Sprout. God gives us good things—food and clothes and a place to live. When we grumble and aren't happy with what we have, that is a sin. But, Sprout, you are not the only one to grumble. We all do at times. Everyone sins. That's why God sent Jesus. Jesus died on the cross for all our sins, even our sins of grumbling and not being happy with what God gives us.

Sprout: Oh, that makes me happy! I'm going to ask Jesus to forgive me for grumbling and give me a thankful heart. And tonight I'm going to take two whole bites of broccoli!

Teacher: That sounds like a good plan, Sprout! God will forgive you, and He will help you be thankful for His good gifts too.

Craft Time

What you do: Hand out Craft Page 10, stickers from the Sticker Page, and scissors for children to make an accordion book. If you teach younger children, you may want to assemble the books ahead of time.

To assemble the books, cut the page in half along the solid line. Tape the two picture strips together. Starting with the picture of the crossing of the Red Sea, fold back and forth on the dotted lines. You will have a series of Bible story pictures on one side and a series of pictures depicting God's care for us on the other side. *Option:* Cut and fold the book for younger children before class.

Hand out the Craft Page to each child and have them follow along as you read the text on each picture and the direction for what to do, one scene at a time. Have them color the scenes and add tent and bird stickers.

Then read the words and directions on the other side. Give children stickers of a Bible, a shirt, and shoes to put on this side. Talk about all the blessings God provides for us, especially the gift of forgiveness He gives us through Jesus' death and resurrection.

Option: If you have time, take a field trip to your sanctuary. Ask your pastor or an elder to meet with the children for a few moments to talk about what happens during the Lord's Supper. Show the children the bread. Show the children the cup. They may wish to touch the chalice. Talk about these good gifts of God and the forgiveness God provides in them.

Growing in CHRIST.

Paper Plus option: Make a "God Cares for Us" hanging. Copy Activity Page 10B for each child. Have children color the pictures and cut them apart. Talk about all the ways God cares for us. Have children use glue to outline a large heart on a piece of construction paper. Add yarn to the glue, and allow it to dry. When it is dry, have them glue the pictures inside the heart to make a collage. They can glue a paper cross or one made from pipe cleaners over the picture. String yarn through the top for hanging.

Snack Time

What you do: Serve water and Nilla wafers. Have children pretend that these yummy cookies are manna. Spread a blanket or tablecloth on the ground and put Nilla wafers on it. Give each child a small cup to pick up five cookies. Tell the children to pretend they are the Israelites picking up manna for breakfast.

Live It Out

Help the children learn to share and show Christian love by making soup together to deliver to some homebound members of your congregation. Talk to your pastor or a member of the human care board for names of these people.

Ask each child to bring in a hard vegetable to contribute to the soup pot. Give each child a paper towel. Let the children take turns peeling the vegetables with a vegetable peeler. If you have enough helpers to supervise, let children also cut the vegetables with a butter knife. It will take the children quite a long time to peel and cut. Enlist additional helpers, but let the children do as much as they are able to do. Place the vegetables in a slow cooker with purchased beef or chicken broth. Tell the children that God loves us and helps us to show love to others.

4 Closing (5 minutes)

Going Home

What you do: Gather take-home items to distribute.

Sing "Thank You, Loving Father" (*LOSP*, p. 71; CD 17) or "God Is So Good" (*LOSP*, p. 57; CD 8) again

Say **Today we learned that God provides all that we need. He gives us food to eat and clothes to wear. He forgives our sins for Jesus' sake and promises in His Word to take us to heaven someday. That's the best gift of all. Let's say "God provides for me" together.** Do so.

Pray **Dear God, thank You for Jesus and for the Bible, where you tell us You love us. Thank You for forgiving our sins. Thank You for taking care of us and giving us what we need. Amen.**

Reflection

Did the children grasp the concept that God is always with them and provides what they need to live? Were they able to express that God's forgiveness through Jesus is God's best blessing?

Lesson 10

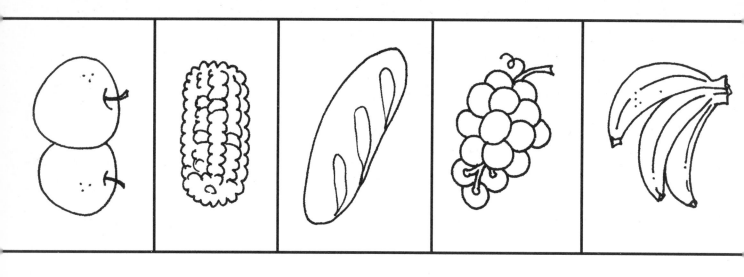

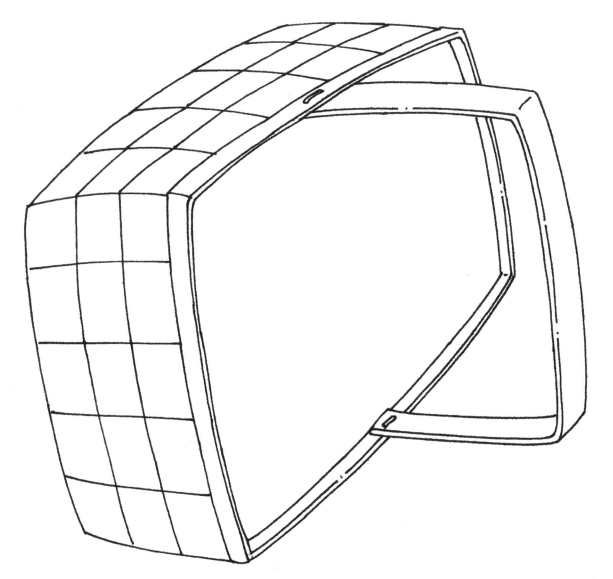

God gives us what we need!

Preparing the Lesson

The Ten Commandments

Exodus 19–20

Date of Use

Key Point

The Law kills, but the Gospel revives. "For the law was given through Moses; grace and truth came through Jesus Christ" (John 1:17).

Law/**Gospel**

The Ten Commandments define God's Law. **Jesus, through His incarnation and by His suffering and death for my sins, defines God's love and mercy toward me.**

Context

In the burning bush, God answers Moses' question, saying, "When you have brought the people out of Egypt, you shall serve God on this mountain" (Exodus 3:12). God fulfills this promise and delivers the Israelites to the base of Mount Sinai. Here, in the midst of the smoldering smoke that shrouds the summit, God gives Moses the Ten Commandments.

Commentary

After parting the seas for us, showering us with manna from heaven, and bringing forth water from a rock to quench our thirst, the Lord prepares to give us a far superior gift. "Let them . . . be ready for the third day" (Exodus 19:10–11), because the Law is coming.

The great cloud descends first "like the smoke of a kiln" (Exodus 19:18), blocking out the light and obscuring our view. Next, we hear the deafening trumpet of God Himself purifying the air before His holy presence. At the sound, the soldiers lift their spears, ready to carry out the Lord's orders. Should a person's hand or foot touch the mountain, "he shall not live" (Exodus 19:13). Our eardrums nearly burst from the thunderclaps as lightning flashes threateningly all around us. Last, God's condemning voice rains vocal death on us in the proclamation of the Ten Commandments. Fear chills the very marrow of our shaking souls as we realize that we can never keep such holy commands.

Through the haze of our singed, stinging, and tear-filled eyes, we see an unassuming figure step forward through the cowering crowd. His broken and bruised back, anointed by the bloodied whip, bears our Law-demanded cross. As He steps on that mountain in our stead, He willingly acquires our death sentence. The soldiers carry out God's command, crucifying Christ. This "man of sorrows" (Isaiah 53:3) pours out His soul to death and is numbered with the transgressors (Isaiah 53:12). The mountains tremble, a cloud of darkness descends, and a soldier spears the One who came not "to abolish the Law or the Prophets" but "to fulfill them" (Matthew 5:17).

Indeed, let us be ready for the third day. The Law kills, but the Gospel revives. When the final earthquakes of the Law reverberate and die on that third day, a tomb sits empty. At this tomb, His angel soothes our ears with His peace-packed proclamation: "Do not be afraid. . . . He is not here, for He has risen, as He said" (Matthew 28:5–6).

While "the law was given through Moses, grace and truth came through Jesus Christ" (John 1:17). Tears of fear melt into joy. May we always live in Christ, through whom "everyone who believes is freed from everything from which you could not be freed by the law of Moses" (Acts 13:38–39).

To hear an in-depth discussion of this Bible account, visit cph.org/podcast and listen to our Seeds of Faith podcast each week.

Lesson 11

The Ten Commandments

Exodus 19–20

Connections

Bible Words
The law was given through Moses; grace and truth came through Jesus Christ. John 1:17

Faith Word
Law

Hymn
O Sing to the Lord (*LSB* 808; CD 2)

Catechism
The Ten Commandments

Take-Home Promise
Jesus kept God's Law for me and paid for my sins on the cross.

1 Opening (15 minutes)

Welcome Time

What you do: Before class, set up two activity areas. In one, put out copies of Activity Page 11B and crayons or markers. Make copies of Activity Page Fun (below and on CD) for parents or classroom helpers.

In the other activity area, clear space to play Red Light, Green Light, or set out red, green, and yellow play dough or copies of Activity Page 11A and glue sticks for each child. Cut red, green, and yellow circles to cover the circles on the stoplight.

Say   Hi, [Dominic]. Good to see you! I wonder . . . how did you get here today? Did you come in your car? Did you walk? Did you have to stop at a red light? We're going to talk about stoplights and rules today.

Direct children to the tables where you have the activities. Encourage parents or caregivers to stay and do the welcome activity with their child.

Activity Page Fun Get a copy of Activity Page 11B and crayons. Have your child count the items in each line, circle the correct number, and color the page.

Say   Today you'll here about ten special rules that God gives us. These rules are called the Ten Commandments.

MATERIALS NEEDED

1 Opening	2 God Speaks	3 We Live	4 Closing
Teacher Tools Attendance chart CD	**Teacher Tools** CD	**Student Pack** Craft Page 11 Stickers	**Teacher Tools** CD
Student Pack Attendance sticker	**Student Pack** Lesson Leaflet 11 Sticker	**Other Supplies** Picture of Jesus or cross Gift bags Traditional twist pretzels Paper Plus supplies (optional)	**Student Pack** Take-home materials
Other Supplies Activity Pages 11A & 11B (TG) Resource Page 1 (TG) Colored paper or play dough (optional)	**Other Supplies** Activity Pages 11A & 11C Cross *The Ten Commandments* Arch Book (optional)		**Other Supplies** Activity Page 11C Cross

Active Learning Play the game Red Light, Green Light. Have children line up.

Say Let's pretend we're driving cars. **What does a red light mean? Stop! What does a green light mean? Go. When I say, "Green light," start driving your car. When I call out, "Red light," stop.** Play the game. Discuss.

Say **Rules are good. They help to keep us safe. Today you will hear about the special rules God gives us. They are called the Ten Commandments.**

Option: Cut red, green, and yellow circles. Have children glue the circles to a piece of paper to make a stoplight, or give the children red, green, and yellow play dough to make stoplights.

Use your classroom signal to let the children know it's time to clean up and gather for circle time. Sing a cleanup song (Resource Page 1).

Gathering in God's Name

What you do: Use this opening format each week so that children become familiar with it. To teach about the Church Year, use the materials in the Church Year Worship Kit (see the introduction for more information).

Sing "Won't You Come and Sit with Me" (*LOSP*, p. 11; CD 18) or another song

Have the children say the Invocation and Amen with you. Tell them "Amen" is the special word they get to say at the end of prayers, hymns, and the like.

Begin **In the name of the Father and of the Son and of the Holy Spirit. Amen.**

Offering Have a child bring the offering basket forward. Sing an offering song.

Pray **Dear God, we are glad to be in Sunday School today to learn about You. Thank You for** [name each child]. **Help us to listen. Help us to speak kind words today. Help us to learn more about how much You love us. For Jesus' sake. Amen.**

Celebrate Birthdays, Baptism birthdays, and special occasions

2 God Speaks (20 minutes)

Story Clue

What you do: Make two copies of Activity Page 11A. Color the light on one green; color the light on the other one red. Tape the pages back to back. Begin with the stoplight that shows the red circle. *Option:* Find pictures online of stoplights with red and green lights to show.

Ask **What does this look like, friends?** If they do not recognize it, tell them it is a stoplight. **When we are driving in our car or walking on the street and the stoplight turns red, what are we supposed to do?**

Show other side. **When the stoplight turns green, what can we do? What happens if we don't obey the stoplight?** Talk about how rules are good because they help to keep us safe.

Say **Today we'll learn about ten special rules that God gives us. Do you know what God's rules are called?** (The Ten Commandments)

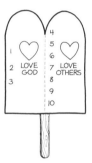

Key Point

The Law kills, but
the Gospel revives.
"For the law was
given through Moses;
grace and truth came
through Jesus Christ"
(John 1:17).

Bible Story Time

What you do: Play the story on track 24 of CD, or tell the story using the following script. Make two story props, one of the stone tablets and the other of Moses' face. For the stone tablets, copy Activity Page 11C, and tape or glue it to poster board. Cut around the tablets and glue them to a jumbo craft stick, ruler, or paint stirrer. Draw Moses' face on a paper plate and attach it to a different stick.

Say **God's people, the Israelites, were camping at the bottom of Mount Sinai. One day, Moses climbed up the mountain to talk to God.** Make Moses puppet "walk" up a mountain. **God said, "I saved My people from bad king Pharaoh. I took care of them in the desert and gave them food and water. I love them. I want them to be My special people. Tell the people to get ready because I want to talk to them."**

So, Moses went back down the mountain to tell the people what God said. Walk puppet down mountain. **Not long after that, there was thunder and lightning and thick smoke over the mountain. Then the people heard a loud trumpet blast, and they felt the mountain shake. This is how God showed the people He was there. The people were afraid, so Moses climbed up the mountain by himself to talk to God.** Walk puppet back up mountain.

God told Moses, "I am the Lord your God who saved you from the Egyptians." Then God gave Moses ten rules, or commandments, that He wanted His people to obey. Here are the commandments God gave. Hold up a finger for each commandment you name.

1. **You shall have no other gods. This means that we should love and trust in God more than anything or anyone else.**

2. **You shall not misuse the name of the Lord your God. God doesn't want us to say bad words; we should use God's name only when we are talking to and about Him.**

3. **Remember the Sabbath (SAB bahth) day by keeping it holy. God wants us to go to church to hear God's Word and worship Him.**

4. **Honor your father and your mother. God wants us to love and be kind to our fathers and mothers. He wants us treat all those who are in charge of us in a kind way and do what they say.**

5. **You shall not murder. God doesn't want us to hurt others.**

6. **You shall not commit adultery. This means that husbands and wives should love and respect each other.**

7. **You shall not steal. Stealing is taking things that don't belong to us. God doesn't want us to do that. He also wants us to help others keep their things safe.**

8. **You shall not give false testimony against your neighbor. Those are big words, aren't they? They mean that God wants us to always tell the truth. We shouldn't talk in a mean way about others, but we should say kind things.**

9 and 10. **You shall not covet your neighbor's house. You shall not covet your neighbor's wife, or his manservant or maidservant, his ox or donkey, or any thing that belongs to your neighbor. God doesn't want us to try to get other people's things. He wants us to be happy with what we have.**

God wrote these rules on two pieces of flat stone. Show the stone tablets. **Moses carried the stones down the mountain and read them to the people.** Walk puppet down mountain. **Now the Israelites knew what God wanted them to do. These rules from God are called the Ten Commandments.** Show tablets again. **We also call them God's Law.**

God's Law tells us how God wants us to live together in love. It shows us the good things to do and say and think and the bad things God does not want us to do or say or think. God's Law is good, but we aren't. Even when we try our best not to do anything wrong but only do the good things God wants, we mess up. Doing things that are wrong and not doing the good things God wants is called sin. No matter how hard we try, we always end up sinning.

But God gives us Good News! Because He loves us, He sent Jesus to be our Savior. Jesus kept God's commandments perfectly for us and took the punishment for our sins by dying on the cross and rising again.

(Ten Commandments from *Luther's Small Catechism with Explanation* © 1986, 1991 CPH.)

Bible Story Review

What you do: Hand out Lesson Leaflet 11, stickers, and crayons or markers. Show the picture on the leaflet and review the story using the questions. Talk about the pictures in the sidebar, and have the children add a sticker to the stone tablets. On the back, connect the dots from 1 to 10 on each commandment.

Option: Use the Arch Book *The Ten Commandments* (CPH, 59-1586) to review.

Ask **Who is on the rock?** Moses

What will God give Moses? The Ten Commandments

Who kept God's law perfectly for you? Jesus

Let the children stand and stretch. Tell them to watch you and hold up fingers as you count and sing "The Ten Commandments" (tune: "Ten Little Indians")

Sing **1 little, 2 little, 3 commandments,**
4 little, 5 little, 6 commandments,
7 little, 8 little, 9 commandments,
10 commandments giv'n by God!

Bible Words

What you do: Read the verse from your Bible. Use the Ten Commandments story prop (Activity Page 11C) and a cross as visuals for the Law and Jesus.

Ask **Are you afraid of thunder and lightning? God's people were afraid when they heard the thunder and saw the mountain smoke and shake. But you know what? They didn't have to be afraid! God loved them. He was giving them a good gift, the Ten Commandments.** Show Activity Page 11C.

When we sin and do bad things, we might be afraid too. Maybe we are afraid that we will be punished for being bad. But God saves us through Jesus, who came to die for our sins. Show cross. **The Bible says** (read verse)**: "The law** (hold up Commandments) **was given through Moses; grace and truth came through Jesus Christ** (hold up cross)."

Let's divide into two groups to learn these words. Group 1 will say the first half; group 2 will say the last half. Then we'll switch. Do this.

③ We Live (20 minutes)

Use these activities to help the children grow in their understanding of what the Bible story means for their lives. Choose the ones that work best with your class.

Growing through God's Word

What you do: Put the stone tablets you made for the story in a gift bag. Put a picture of Jesus or a cross in another gift bag. You will also need Craft Page 11.

Say **Rules help to keep us safe. What are some rules you have at your house? What are some rules you have at preschool?** Spend time talking about rules.

Because God loves us, He gave us special rules too. What are the rules that God gives us called? Hold up the tablets of stone. **God's rules are called the Ten Commandments. The Commandments are also called God's Law. God's Law is good. It is a gift from God. It tells us how God wants us to live together in love. God wants us to do all the things He tells us to do in His Law all the time.**

What are some things God wants us to do? Let children tell what they remember.

Then point to the pictures on side 2 of the Craft Page. Point out the children who are keeping the commandments (the child who is praying, the children obeying their parents, etc.).

Ask **Do we do all those things? No, we don't.**

Say **God's Law shows us that we do wrong things. We are sinful. Sometimes we don't want to go to church. Sometimes we say a mean thing to our friend. Sometimes we tell our mom or dad "no."** Help the children think about ways they don't do what God wants. **All those things are sins. They are ways we don't keep God's Law the way He wants us to.**

Hold up gift bag that you took tablets out of. **The Bible tells us about God's Law. It is a good gift. But we aren't good. That's why God gives us another good gift.**

Ask **Do you know what this gift is?** Accept answers, then hold up other gift bag and take out cross or picture of Jesus.

Say **This gift is called the Gospel. The Gospel is Good News. It tells us that even though we can't keep God's Law and deserve to be punished, we aren't! That's because Jesus loves us so much that He came to take our punishment on the cross. Because of Jesus, God forgives our sins.**

Craft Time

What you do: You will need Craft Page 11 and the stickers from the Sticker Page. For younger children, cut around the curved line and fold along the dark line to make it easier for them to use.

Show the mountain side of the page first. Have the children color the picture. Ask children about the scene. Then have them fold up the curved part on the fold line. Talk about the rest of the story. Give the children a sticker of the commandments to add to Moses' arms.

Growing in CHRisT.

On side 2, have the children put commandment stickers by the pictures showing children keeping the commandments and mark a cross over those who are not. Then finish the dot-to-dot cross.

Ask **Which children need God's forgiveness?** All of them! **Draw lines from the cross to all the children.**

Only Jesus has kept the Law perfectly. We all need God's forgiveness. It is also through the Gospel that God gives power to strive to live according to the Law.

Paper Plus option: Copy Activity Page 11C for each child. Children should cut around the outline and color the tablets. Give each child a small cup of popcorn, round stickers, or O-shaped cereal. Help the children glue the correct number of items next to each number to make a number chart.

Snack Time

What you do: Count out ten hug-shaped pretzels for each child. Talk about the Ten Commandments God gave Moses. Hug self. Say the pretzels can remind us of God's love because they look like hugs. The Commandments show us how God wants us to love others. But we can't keep them. So, God, out of love, sent Jesus to be our Savior. He kept all of the Commandments for us and then died on the cross to pay for our sins.

Live It Out

Help the children learn to respect and appreciate authority. Have them make cards to mail to your local police office, thanking them for helping to keep people safe by enforcing the rules designed to protect us.

Faith in Action!

4 Closing (5 minutes)

2, 10

Going Home

What you do: Gather all the take-home materials. Show Ten Commandments story prop (Activity Page 11C) and cross.

Sing "O Sing to the Lord" (*LSB* 808; CD 2) or "God Loves Me Dearly" (*LOSP*, p. 85; CD 10)

Say **God gave us the Ten Commandments because He loves us. They are God's Law.** Show Commandments. **They tell us how to love God and others. But we can't do what God wants. We sin. So, God sent Jesus to save us from our sins.** Show cross. **Jesus kept all of God's rules for us. Then He took our punishment on the cross! This Good News is called the Gospel!**

Let's say "Jesus kept God's Law for me and paid for my sins on the cross" together. Do so.

Pray **Dear God, thank You for giving us the Ten Commandments to show us how to live in love. Thank You for sending Jesus to obey Your commandments for us and to take the punishment for what we do wrong. Amen.**

Reflection

Do you need to provide more opportunities for movement? Repeat favorite transition activities from week to week.

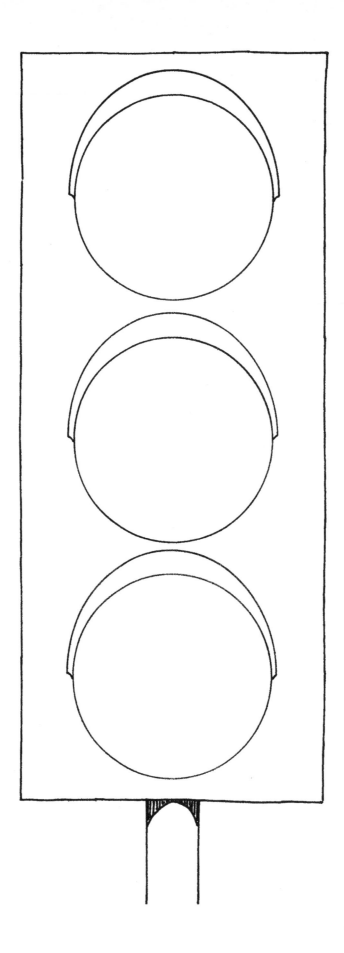

Count how many, and circle the correct number.

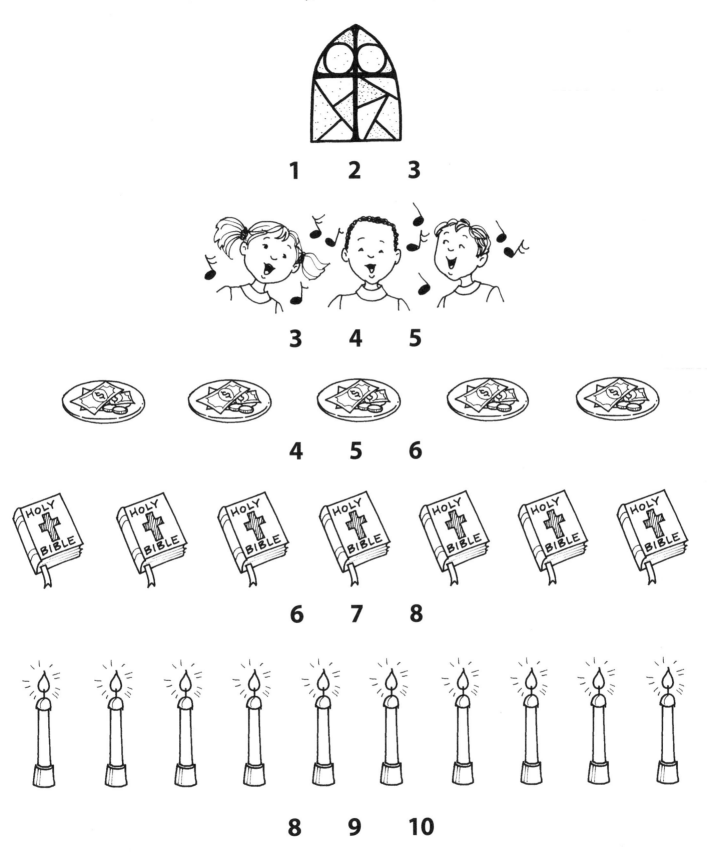

1   2   3

3   4   5

4   5   6

6   7   8

8   9   10

1

2

3

Love
God

4

5

6

7

8

9

10

Love
Others

Preparing the Lesson

Worship in the Tabernacle

Exodus 40

Date of Use

Key Point

In the tabernacle, God dwelled with His people, cleansing them and making them holy through the blood of sacrifices. In Christ, God now dwells among us, cleansing us and making us holy through Jesus' blood, shed for us on the cross.

Law/**Gospel**

My sin makes me unholy and separates me from God; I am unworthy to stand in His presence. **God cleanses me, makes me holy, and dwells in me through the once-for-all sacrifice of Christ.**

Context

The Israelites are camped at Sinai, almost a year after their exodus from Egypt. The Ten Commandments have been received . . . and almost immediately shattered when the golden calf is constructed. But God has provided a means of atonement for the people: the altar and blood of sacrifice.

The Lord has shown Moses a heavenly tabernacle after which he is to model the earthly tabernacle. Earth reflects heaven. Indeed, heaven is present on earth as the heavenly Lord takes up residence within the tabernacle. Afterward, as recorded in Leviticus, the Lord will institute the various sacrifices by which He will maintain fellowship with His nation.

Commentary

Eden was a sanctuary of sorts, where humans lived and worked in perfect communion with God. But in the post-Eden world, where death and sin strangled creation, where were humans to turn? Where was the "Eden" where they could be made right with God? The Lord made a new garden. The tabernacle became this new Eden for all fallen Adams and Eves. Here, they could return to the Lord and be purified and made holy through the bloody sacrifices instituted by God for their sake. The place even had the look of a garden, with various flora and fauna woven into the very fabric of the tent. Everything about the sanctuary visually proclaimed, "Welcome home, sons of Adam and daughters of Eve! Welcome back to Eden!"

As Eden opened on the east (Genesis 3:24), so did the tabernacle. There, Israelites reentered God's holy place via the altar, and *only* via the altar. There, the blood of bulls, goats, sheep, and doves was poured out. This blood was not simple blood, but blood ordained by God through His Word. God did not need it; sinners did. The sacrifices were for their benefit. By it, they were cleaned, renewed, and made holy.

God's dwelling within the tabernacle also foreshadowed a future, more intimate dwelling of God among people. For the Word became flesh and dwelt (literally, "tabernacled") among us (John 1:14). The Son made our flesh His own; the Creator assumed the stuff of His own creation. His body is our tabernacle, holy and pure.

Baptized into His pure and holy body, we are pure and holy also. We enter where no Old Testament high priest ever could: into the body of God Himself. He cleanses and sanctifies us. Through His once-for-all sacrifice, we are welcomed back into a new Eden: the Church.

Exodus 40 stresses that Moses made everything exactly as God instructed him. Nothing was done willy-nilly; for just as everything in creation had its right place, so in this place of new creation, everything had its right place. For here, God re-created fallen sinners, refashioned them in His image, and restored them to fellowship with Him. In doing all this, He gave an ongoing preview of what He would do in His Son, who is our Tabernacle, our Priest, our Sacrifice, and our Holiness.

To hear an in-depth discussion of this Bible account, visit cph.org/podcast and listen to our Seeds of Faith podcast each week.

Lesson 12

Worship in the Tabernacle

Exodus 40

Connections

Bible Words
Oh give thanks to the LORD, for He is good. Psalm 107:1 (CD 6)

Faith Word
Tabernacle

Hymn
O Sing to the Lord (*LSB* 808; CD 2)

Catechism
Lord's Prayer

Take-Home Promise
Jesus is with me.

1 Opening (15 minutes)

Welcome Time

What you do: Before class, set up two activity areas. In one, put out copies of Activity Page 12A, "five senses" stickers (Sticker Sheet), and crayons. Make copies of Activity Page Fun (below and on CD) for parents or classroom helpers.

In the other activity area, set out chairs, hymnals, a Bible, candles, an offering plate or basket, a basin for a baptismal font, a doll, and other items so the children can act out things we do in worship.

Say **Hi, [Lila]. I wonder . . . did you go to church already? Today, we're going to find out about a special church God's people in the Bible built.**

Direct children to the tables where you have the activities. Encourage parents or caregivers to stay and do the welcome activity with their child.

Activity Page Fun Get a copy of Activity Page 12A, stickers, and crayons. Color the page together and talk about things you see, hear, touch, taste, and smell in church. Then give your child stickers to put on or near those things.

Say **Here are some stickers. Put the eyes on things you see in church. Now put the ears on things you hear in church** (e.g., a choir). **What is something people taste in church?** (Lord's Supper) **Put a tongue there. There are two stickers left. Put the hand on something you touch** (e.g., a hymnal). **Find something you smell in church** (e.g., candles, flowers). **Put the nose there.**

Today you'll hear about a special church God's people built to worship Him. Listen for the name of it. You can tell me after Sunday School.

© 2015 Concordia Publishing House. Reproduced by permission. Available on the Teacher CD.

MATERIALS NEEDED

1 Opening	2 God Speaks	3 We Live	4 Closing
Teacher Tools Attendance chart CD	**Teacher Tools** Figures 12-1 to 12-8 Background A Poster F CD	**Student Pack** Craft Page 12 Stickers	**Teacher Tools** CD
Student Pack Attendance sticker Activity Page stickers	**Student Pack** Lesson Leaflet 12 Stickers	**Other Supplies** Sprout Pictures of church items Yarn or ribbon & decorating supplies Graham crackers & frosting or cheese Paper Plus supplies (optional)	**Student Pack** Take-home items
Other Supplies Activity Page 12A (TG) Church items Resource Page 1 (TG)	**Other Supplies** Sprout Blocks, towel, paper cups (optional)		

Active Learning Begin with the finger play; then, encourage children to "play" church with the items you've set out. Observe what they do to gain insights into their worship experiences and ways you can give instruction.

Ask **Can you do this with me?** Let children practice interlocking their fingers upside down. Then lead them in this familiar rhyme.

Say **Here is the church** Interlock fingers upside down.
Here is the steeple. Hold up pointer fingers.
Open the doors Open thumbs.
And see all the people. Wiggle fingers.

Say **It is good to go to church to worship God! Pretend you are in church now. What do you see? What do you do?**

Use your classroom signal to let the children know it's time to clean up and gather for circle time. Sing a cleanup song (Resource Page 1).

Gathering in God's Name

What you do: Use this opening format each week so that children become familiar with it. To teach about the Church Year, use the materials in the Church Year Worship Kit (see the introduction for more information).

Sing "Won't You Come and Sit with Me" (*LOSP*, p. 11; CD 18) or another song

Have the children say the Invocation and Amen with you. Tell them "Amen" is the special word they get to say at the end of prayers, hymns, and the like.

Begin **In the name of the Father and of the Son and of the Holy Spirit. Amen.**

Offering Have a child bring the offering basket forward. Sing an offering song.

Pray **Dear heavenly Father, we are glad to be here today to learn more about You. Help us to listen and show love. Thank You for sending Jesus to be our Savior. Amen.**

Celebrate Birthdays, Baptism birthdays, and special occasions

2 God Speaks (20 minutes)

Story Clue

What you do: Use Sprout or another puppet and your Bible.

Teacher: Boys and girls, Sprout is here again today. Let's welcome him by saying hello. (*Look at puppet.*) Hello, Sprout!

Sprout: Hi, everybody! It's gr-r-reat to be here. I love Sunday School!

Teacher: Me too, Sprout! We get to be with our friends and learn about God from His Word, the Bible. (*Show Bible.*) The Bible is very special because God wrote it.

Sprout: I love to hear about Jesus! And after Sunday School, I'm going to church!

Teacher: Yes, it's a great blessing to have a church where we can worship God.

Sprout: It sure is! Last Sunday, the pastor baptized a little baby. Then we all got to welcome the baby as part of God's family. I can't wait until she gets big enough to come to Sunday School too.

Teacher: God does lots of special things for us in church. He makes us His children through Holy Baptism. He talks to us in His Word and tells us how He sent Jesus

Key Point

In the tabernacle, God dwelled with His people, cleansing them and making them holy through the blood of sacrifices. In Christ, God now dwells among us, cleansing us and making us holy through Jesus' blood, shed for us on the cross.

Great Idea!

to save us from our sins—all the wrong things we think and say and do!

Sprout: Yeah, and we get to sing and pray and give God our offerings too!

Teacher: I'm glad we have a church. But did you know that a long time ago, God's people didn't have a place to worship God?

Sprout: (*Surprised*) They didn't?

Teacher: No, not until God told Moses to build a tabernacle.

Sprout: What's a ta-burr-knuckel?

Teacher: Tabernacle. The tabernacle was a special place a little like our church. Would you like to learn more about it? Sit over here, and you can listen while I tell this true story about the tabernacle from God's Word. (*Set Sprout down.*)

Bible Story Time

What you do: Use Background A, the story figures for Lesson 12, and the tent on Poster F. Use a restickable glue stick (see Introduction for more information), double-sided tape, or loops of tape to attach the figures to the background.

Option: Stack blocks in a rectangular shape to represent the tabernacle. Leave an opening for the entrance. Attach the story figures to upside-down paper cups. Place them in the tabernacle as you tell the story. Use a white dish towel for the cloud. Gather the children around you so they can see.

Say **This true story from the Bible happened after God's people had left Egypt and were living in the wilderness. Their leader, Moses, had gone to the top of Mount Sinai. God spoke to Moses there and gave His people the Ten Commandments. God told them, "I love you. I am your God and you are My children."**

One day, God talked to Moses again. Show Moses (12-1). **He said, "Moses, I want My people to know how much I love them. Build a special place for Me where I can live with them and they can worship Me."**

Then God gave Moses directions for how to build His special home. He told Moses to put up a big tent and hang a curtain in it. Put the curtain from Poster F on Background A, or stack blocks in a rectangle.

Next, God told Moses to put special things in the big tent. He said, "Put the ark of the covenant behind the curtain." Put ark (12-2) on the background or inside your block tabernacle. **The ark was a beautiful box covered with gold. It held the Ten Commandments and other special church things.** Add following figures as you name them.

Then God told Moses to put a lampstand (12-3), a table with bread (12-4), and an altar of incense in the tent (12-5).

Next, God told Moses to put a basin of water in the tent. Add basin (12-6). **Now Moses and the priests could wash themselves so they would be clean when they served inside God's house. Near the door of the tent, God told Moses to put an altar for sacrifices.** Add bronze altar (12-7).

Moses did all the things God said to do. The special tent was called a tabernacle.

Ask **Can you say that with me?** Lead children in saying "tabernacle."

Say **Then a big cloud covered the tabernacle. And do you know what?** Whisper slowly: **God was in the cloud!** Add cloud (12-8) to the background, or cover the block tabernacle with the white towel.

Growing in CHRIST.

This special cloud filled the tabernacle during the day. When night came, a fire burned inside the cloud. This is how God showed He was with His people, no matter what. When God wanted His people to move, He led the way in the cloud. The tabernacle was the special place where God lived with His people.

Ask What do we call the special place where God meets us and we worship Him? Church

Say The church is God's house. When we go to church, we can be sure Jesus is there with us too. He is there in His Word and Holy Baptism and the Lord's Supper to forgive our sins and help us grow as His children.

Bible Story Review

What you do: Hand out Lesson Leaflet 12 and crayons. Point to the Bible story picture on the leaflet and show the storytelling figures to review the story.

Ask What are the people doing? They are building the tabernacle. God told them to do this so they would know that God was with them.

What special things does God tell them to put in the tabernacle? Help the children name the items in the picture or show the storytelling figures.

Who will live in the tabernacle? God

What special things are in your church? Accept answers.

Point to Moses and have children connect the dots to make the stone tablets. Look at the Bible art and sidebar pictures.

Say Connect the dots. What is Moses holding? Ten Commandments **Now look at the pictures in the box.** Point to sidebar pictures. **What are they? Which ones did God tell Moses to put in the tabernacle (tent-church)? Look for them in the Bible picture; then color them here. Which one do you see in our church? Circle it. Who died on a cross for you? Jesus!**

Do the "Here Is the Church" finger play together again. Encourage children to do this for their grown-ups at home and draw people in the church.

Bible Words

What you do: Read the Bible Words from Psalm 107:1 in your Bible. Play track 6 of the CD, or use the action poem to help the children learn the words.

Say God was with His people in the special tent-church and forgave their sins. They were thankful for God's love and forgiveness.

Ask What do you think they told God? Accept answers.

Say Maybe they said something like this: "Oh give thanks to the Lord, for He is good." These words come from Psalm 107:1 in the Bible.

Say In His Word, God tells us that He sent Jesus to earth to be with us and save us from our sins. In Holy Baptism, God the Holy Spirit comes to live in us and make us God's children. He forgives our sins and makes us holy.

That makes us thankful too! We can say the Bible Words too: "Oh give thanks to the Lord, for He is good." Let's listen to the Bible Words song. Then we'll sing along. Play track 6 on the CD.

Option: Say the "Thank You Litany" (*Wiggle & Wonder*, p. 15) to help the children learn the Bible Words.

③ We Live (20 minutes)

Use these activities to help the children grow in their understanding of what the Bible story means for their lives. Choose the ones that work best with your class.

Growing through God's Word

What you do: Before class, go to the sanctuary and take pictures of the altar candles, altar, cross, baptismal font, Bible, and Communionware on your tablet device, or find pictures online or in a book. Show the pictures to the children when you talk about the things we see in church with Sprout.

Option: Take the children on a field trip to your church sanctuary. Ask what they see (e.g., stained-glass windows, candles, altar, lectern, pulpit, font, crucifix). Ask your pastor or an altar guild member to talk about these special things.

Sprout: God's house sure looked different a long time ago!

Teacher: Yes, it was a big tent! That way, God's people could take their church with them as they traveled to the Promised Land. We don't usually worship God in a tent, but we have special things in our church too. Some of the things are a bit like the things in the tabernacle tent-church. For instance, we have candles. (*Show the candelabrum.*) What else do we have in church?

Sprout: Umm . . . an altar?

Teacher: Yes, God told Moses to put an altar in the tabernacle. We have an altar in our church too. (*Show altar.*) Our altar reminds us that God sent Jesus to be our Savior. He died on the cross for us to save us from our sins. (*Show cross.*)

Sprout: And they had a basin of water. We do too!

Teacher: You are right. The tabernacle had a basin of water for the priests to wash their hands so they would be clean in God's house. (*Show font.*) We have a baptismal font where God washes away our sins and makes us His children.

Sprout: What about the Bible? Did they have that?

Teacher: Oh, yes! Remember, they had God's Word, the Ten Commandments on tablets of stone. It was kept in a special box called the ark of the covenant. In our church, the pastor teaches us from God's Word, the Bible. (*Show Bible.*)

Sprout: (*Scratching head*) I can't think of anything else.

Teacher: Well, God's people had a special table with bread on it. (*Show plate and chalice.*) We get bread and wine in the Lord's Supper for forgiveness.

Sprout: Wow! God sure loves us a lot! That makes me want to say thank You to God and tell Him how great He is. We get to do that in church too, don't we?

Teacher: We sure do. Because we belong to Jesus, we can sing and praise God. We can pray to God and know He will answer our prayers in a way that is best. We can give Him our offerings so others will learn about Him.

Sprout: I want everyone to know about Jesus! I'm going to ask my friend Rosa to come to church with me next week! I want her to hear about Jesus!

Teacher: That's a great idea, Sprout! God wants everyone to hear that Jesus came to be our Savior from sin. Let's sing about that.

Sing "Come and Go with Me" (*LOSP,* p. 99).

Growing in CHRIST

Craft Time

What you do: Use Craft Page 12, stickers, markers, yarn or ribbon, tissue paper, and other decorating materials to make a banner. The banner can remind the children of God's love in Jesus and the gifts God gives when we gather in His house to worship Him. Follow the directions on the Craft Page to make the banner.

Say **Today we talked about things we see in church. Sometimes we hang banners in church to remind us of Jesus and His love. Today we're going to make a banner that we can hang at home.**

Paper Plus option: Make copies of Activity Page 12B for each child. Give the children yarn, macaroni, or O-shaped cereal to glue to the outline of the church and markers or crayons to color the pictures at the bottom of the page. Cut the pictures apart and glue these inside the church outline. Glue the church to a larger piece of construction paper for durability and a "frame" effect.

Snack Time

What you do: Serve graham crackers churches with crosses made out of frosting or pressurized cheese in a can. Talk about what we see and do in church.

Live It Out

One way we show our thanks for God's blessings is by giving an offering in church or Sunday School. Help the children track their giving using an offering chain. You will need paper strips, tape, and a marker. On the first link in the chain, write the word *blessing*. Each week as the children give their offering, ask them to name one of their blessings. Write the blessing on the strip, and add it to the chain. *Option:* Give the children the paper links at the beginning of class to draw their blessings.

4 Closing (5 minutes)

Going Home

What you do: Gather materials to hand out and have your CD ready to play.

Sing "O Sing to the Lord" (*LSB* 808; CD 2) or "God Loves Me Dearly" (*LOSP*, p. 85; CD 10)

Say **The church is God's house. When we go to church, Jesus is there in His Word and Baptism and Holy Communion to forgive us and helps us grow as His children. He tells us in His Word, "I am with you always." Let's say "Jesus is with me" together.** Do so.

Pray **Dear God, thank You for our church where we hear about You. Thank You for sending Jesus to save us and be with us always. Amen.**

Reflection

How did the lesson go? Spend a few extra minutes on the parts that were more difficult to teach when you prepare for next week's lesson.

What do you see in church? hear? taste? smell? touch?

Things I See in Church

Preparing the Lesson

The Bronze Serpent

Numbers 21:4–9

Date of Use

Key Point

As the bronze serpent was lifted up to heal and save the Israelites from the snakes, so Christ was lifted up on the cross to heal and save us from sin, death, and the devil.

Law/Gospel

Bitten and poisoned by sin and death, I complain when life is not what I want. **God calls me to repentance and points me to Christ, who heals me by His death and resurrection.**

Context

Forty years have passed since the nation began their wanderings as punishment for their rebellion (Numbers 13–14). A new generation is about to be given their chance to enter the Promised Land.

But like father, like son—their mouths are full of murmuring, for their hearts are overflowing with mistrust of God's benevolence. The woebegone desert in which they travel prompts them to throw a national pity party. After this incident, they will prove victor over enemy nations and encamp in the land east of the Jordan to prepare for Moses' farewell sermons (Deuteronomy) and their entry under Joshua's leadership.

Commentary

In Scripture, the snake is the devil's pet. Ever since Satan hissed his lies through that serpentine mouth in Eden, these reptiles have been demonized. Hardly does the Bible have a good word to say about them; in fact, quite the opposite. Even when Moses' and Aaron's staffs are transformed into snakes (Exodus 4:3; 7:9–12), they are hardly treated as "man's best friend."

It comes as no surprise, then, that of all the animals chosen to plague the grumbling, unbelieving Israelites in the desert, snakes were the chosen weapon. These were "fiery serpents," which probably refers not to their appearance (as if they were glowing) but to the effect of their venom on the human body. Not only did it burn, however; it also killed.

This is a radical call to repentance. But as the psalmist says, "When He killed them, they sought Him" (Psalm 78:34). Sometimes, one has to come face-to-face with death to face up to his or her sin and seek the face of the living God. So it was for Israel. So it is oftentimes for us.

The confession of the people is good and right. They have sinned against God and His chosen leader. But what they want is not what they need. They don't need a divine St. Patrick to clear their little desert Ireland of serpents.

Christ knows what they need: a visible conduit for His healing, a medicine that is in the very image of the problem itself. They need a serpent of salvation, and that's what God gives them. The bronze serpent, uplifted on the pole, is the means chosen to grant healing and relief. Under the guise of these deadly serpents, this bronze serpent works not death but life. Through it, Christ saves.

In John 3:14, Jesus says that as Moses raised this serpent in the wilderness, so He, too, must be lifted up on the cross to draw all men to Himself. Hidden under the guise of a condemned sinner is the Holy One of God. He has become our sin, *the* sinner, that we might become the righteousness of God in Him (2 Corinthians 5:21). Christ is our true "serpent of salvation," in whom we are healed from the venom of sin and death.

To hear an in-depth discussion of this Bible account, visit cph.org/podcast and listen to our Seeds of Faith podcast each week.

Lesson 13

The Bronze Serpent

Numbers 21:4–9

Connections

Bible Words
The wages of sin is death, but the free gift of God is eternal life in Christ Jesus. Romans 6:23

Faith Word
Crucifix

Hymn
O Sing to the Lord (*LSB* 808; CD 2)

Catechism
Apostles' Creed:
First & Second Articles

Liturgy
Sign of the cross

Take-Home Promise
Jesus saves me from my sins. He gives me eternal life.

1 Opening (15 minutes)

Welcome Time

What you do: Before class, set up two activity areas. In one, put out copies of Activity Page 13A, stickers (Sticker Sheet), and crayons. Make copies of Activity Page Fun (below and on CD) for parents or helpers.

In the other activity area, set out toy medical kits, a box of bandages, and dolls.

Welcome each child as he or she arrives. Give child a sticker to put on the attendance chart.

Say Hi, [Auggie]. I am happy you are here! I wonder . . . have you ever had to go to the doctor because you were sick or had an owie? How did the doctor help? Today, we will learn about a time when God's people needed help.

Direct children to the tables where you have the activities. Encourage parents or caregivers to stay and do the welcome activity with their child.

Activity Page Fun Get a copy of Activity Page 13A, crayons, and stickers of a bandage and praying hands. Point to child on the Activity Page.

Ask What do you think is wrong with this child? Listen to answers. **How does God help us when we are sick or hurt?** Talk about how God gives us medicine and doctors and people who love us.

Say Draw lines between the child and the things that can help him get better. Here is a bandage. Give child sticker. **Where will you put it? When we are sick, we can talk to God and ask Him to help us. Here are some praying hands to remind you of that.** Give child a sticker.

Today, you'll hear about a time God's people needed help.

MATERIALS NEEDED

1 Opening	2 God Speaks	3 We Live	4 Closing
Teacher Tools Attendance chart CD	**Teacher Tools** CD	**Student Pack** Craft Page 13 Stickers	**Teacher Tools** CD
Student Pack Attendance sticker Activity Page stickers	**Student Pack** Lesson Leaflet 13	**Other Supplies** Sprout Index cards or construction paper Paper Plus supplies (optional) Pretzels & gummy worms	**Student Pack** Take-home items

Other Supplies
Activity Page 13A (TG)
Toy medical kit, bandages, & dolls
Resource Page 1 (TG)
	Other Supplies
	Paper bag or gift bag
	Medical supplies
	Play dough & pencil OR
	  Activity Page 13B & ruler
	Moses and the Bronze Snake
	  Arch Book (optional)
			Other Supplies
			Activity Page 13B (TG)

Active Learning Encourage the children to play hospital with the dolls and toy medical supplies. Talk about ways God gives healing.

Use your classroom signal to let the children know it's time to clean up and gather for circle time. Sing a cleanup song (Resource Page 1).

Gathering in God's Name

What you do: Use this opening format each week so that children become familiar with it. To teach about the Church Year, use the materials in the Church Year Worship Kit (see the introduction for more information).

Sing "Won't You Come and Sit with Me" (*LOSP*, p. 11; CD 18) or another song

Have the children say the Invocation and Amen with you. Tell them "Amen" is the special word they get to say at the end of prayers, hymns, and the like.

Begin **In the name of the Father and of the Son and of the Holy Spirit. Amen.**

Offering Have a child bring the offering basket forward. Sing an offering song.

Pray **Dear God, thank You for taking care of us.** Pray for absent children who are sick or for people the children name who are sick. **Please help [Madelyn and Hayden] get better. Thank You for Jesus, who took away our sin sickness through His death on the cross. Amen.**

Celebrate Birthdays, Baptism birthdays, and special occasions

2 God Speaks (20 minutes)

Story Clue

What you do: In a paper bag or gift bag, place several items that people use when they are sick (e.g., medicine, a heating pad, lip balm, tissues, bandages). Hold up the bag to get the children's attention.

Say **Today I brought some things that I use when I am sick or hurt. What do you think I have?** Accept guesses. **Let's find out if you are right.** Take out the heating pad.

Ask **Hmm. Do you know what this is? What can I use it for?** Accept answers. **I wonder what else is in here.**

Give clues for the children to guess (e.g., I wipe my nose with it; I put it on an owie; I take it when I have a temperature). Take out each item when the children guess correctly. Discuss how each item helps us. Then conclude.

Say **We use these things when we are sick or hurt. God works through them to make us better. Sometimes they make us feel better right away. Sometimes it takes a while to get better, but it is always God who heals us.**

In our Bible story today, God's people are sick, but God doesn't use medicine or doctors to make the sick people better. He uses something surprising! Are you ready to listen so you can find out what it is?

Bible Story Time

What you do: Make a play dough snake, or copy Activity Page 13B. Color and cut out the main snake on the solid lines to make a spiral that looks like a snake uncoiling. During the story, attach the snake you made to a pencil or ruler. Tell the children that this is a true story from the Bible. *Option:* Show the pictures in the Arch book *Moses and the Bronze Snake* (CPH, 59-2219) as you tell the story.

Key Point

As the bronze serpent was lifted up to heal and save the Israelites from the snakes, so Christ was lifted up on the cross to heal and save us from sin, death, and the devil.

Say **God's people, the Israelites, had left Egypt. They were on their way to the new land God promised to give them. But right now, they were wandering in the desert.** Walk in place. **The people were not happy. They wanted to be in their new homes right away. "It's too hot here," they grumbled. "Why did God send Moses to take us out of Egypt? Now, we have to eat the same thing all the time. We're tired of this food!" Grumble, grumble, grumble. The people were not thankful for how God was taking care of them.**

Soon snakes slithered into the camp. The snakes bit the people. Many people got sick and died. Now the people were sorry for grumbling. "Moses!" they called. "We know we were bad. Please pray for us. Ask God to forgive us and save us from the snakes!" So Moses begged God to save His people.

God loved His people very much. He told Moses, "Make a snake out of bronze metal and put it on a pole." So, Moses took a hammer and made a snake out of metal. Make a snake out of play dough, or hold up the paper snake you made. **Then Moses put the snake on the pole.** Wrap your snake around a pencil or ruler, and secure it.

God told Moses, "Tell those who have been bitten by a snake to look at the snake on the pole; then they will get well again." Hold up your snake. **And that's just what happened. Those who looked at the snake on the pole got better. Those who didn't do as God said died. This is how God saved His people.**

Ask **Do you ever grumble? Do you ever whine and say, "I don't like that!"?**

Say **We all grumble and complain. That's because we are sinners. But God saves us from our grumbling sins. He sent Jesus to be our Savior. Jesus was put on a cross where He suffered and died for us. Jesus saves everyone who believes in Him from sin—all the wrong things we think and say and do—and gives us a home in heaven. He is with us now and helps us in our troubles. Someday, we will get to live with Jesus forever.**

Bible Story Review

What you do: Hand out Lesson Leaflet 13 and crayons. Use the questions to review the story, then have the children act it out with you. This will help them understand and remember it better. Finish with the activities on the leaflet, or tell them to do these with grown-ups at home. Begin by showing the leaflet.

Ask **What are the snakes doing?** Biting the people

What does God tell Moses to do to help the sick people? He tells Moses to put a metal snake on a pole for them to look at.

What will happen to the people who look at the snake on the pole? They will get better and live.

Who died on a cross to save you? Jesus

Say **Now let's pretend and act out the story together.** Have children follow your directions and imitate your actions.

Ask **What sound does a snake make?** Ssssssss! Have children make that sound. **Let's pretend we're wiggly snakes.** Show children how to put their hands together and move them in snake motion, or have them wiggle on the ground.

Growing in CHRiST

Now pretend we're God's people walking to a new place to live. Walk in place. **"We're so hot!"** Wipe brow. **"We're so tired!"** Sit down. **"We don't like the desert!"** Shake head no. **Grumble, grumble, grumble.**

Look! There are snakes coming into the camp! Make wiggle motion with hands, or have children wiggle on the ground. **"Ouch! These snakes bite. I feel sick!"** Shake hand; hold tummy. **"Moses, we're sorry! We know we sinned when we grumbled. Ask God to save us!"** Making praying hands.

God told Moses to make a snake out of metal. Pretend to hammer. **Moses said, "Look at the snake on the pole."** Cup hand over eyes and look up. Hold out arms. **"Look, God has made us better!"** Have children sit down.

Now look at your leaflet. Use your finger to find the snake on a pole, the man, and a snake in the Bible story picture. If you find them, color the little pictures. Help children make matches between the pictures. Have them draw a cross in the box, then do the hidden picture on side 2.

Bible Words

What you do: Read the Bible Words from Romans 6:23 in your Bible.

Say   The Bible says, "The wages of sin is death, but the free gift of God is eternal life in Christ Jesus."

Ask   What happened when God's people sinned by grumbling? (Snakes bit many of them and they died.) **What happened when they were sorry and asked God for help?** (God helped them and they lived.)

Say   The snake on the pole reminds us of Jesus on the cross. We sin, too, and deserve to die. But Jesus took away our sins through His death on the cross and gives us eternal life. Let's say our Bible Words together.

Have children join you in saying the words with motions. Do this several times.

Say   **The wages of sin is death,**   Wiggle hands like a snake.
       but the free gift of God   Extend hands, palms up.
       is eternal life   Point up.
       in Christ Jesus.   Make a cross with fingers.

3 We Live (20 minutes)

Use these activities to help the children grow in their understanding of what the Bible story means for their lives. Choose the ones that work best with your class.

Growing through God's Word

What you do: Use Sprout or another puppet. Have him come in running.

Teacher: Sprout, slow down! Where are you going so fast?

Sprout: (*Puffing and running in place*) Well, I was listening to the Bible story . . . When God's people started complaining, snakes came and bit them and made them sick. I'm afraid of snakes! I don't want one to bite me and make me sick! So, I'm running away.

Teacher: (*Holding him still*) I've got good news for you, Sprout. You can stop running. There aren't any snakes here! But . . . why do you think a snake would come and do that anyway? Have you been . . . grumbling?

Sprout: Well (*hanging head*) . . . maybe just a little. But I had a bad day yesterday. First, my mom made me eat eggs for breakfast! I don't like eggs. Then I had to pick up all my toys before I could go outside. That made me grumble. Then for lunch, I had to eat leftovers. Yuck! I hate leftovers! I wanted pizza! Then my mom asked me to help her fold clothes. I had to work and eat yucky food all day long!

Teacher: Oh, Sprout, your grumbling *does* remind me of God's people in our Bible story today! You have food and toys and many other good things, but you still aren't happy with the things God gives you. You want something else.

Sprout: (*Hanging head*) Yeah, I know. Grumbling and not being thankful for what God gives us is a sin, isn't it, teacher?

Teacher: Yes, it is, Sprout. God gives us food and clothes and toys and a place to live. When we grumble and aren't happy with what we have, that is a sin. But, Sprout, you still don't have to worry about snakes biting you.

Sprout: I don't? How come?

Teacher: Because God loves us. Remember how He loved His people in the Bible and made a plan to save them? He had Moses make a snake on a pole. Well, God loves us too. He made a plan to save us from our sins. He sent Jesus to die on the cross for all our sins, even our sins of not being happy with what He gives us.

Sprout: Wow! I'm glad Jesus came to save me. I'm going to tell God I'm sorry for grumbling and ask Him to forgive me. I'm really thankful that I don't have to worry about those snakes!

Teacher: That sounds like a good plan, Sprout! Quit worrying about snakes. God forgives you. He will help you be thankful for His good gifts too.

Craft Time

What you do: Use Craft Page 13 and stickers to make a first-aid kit. You will need index cards or pieces of construction paper cut to fit inside the finished kit.

Say Today, we're going to make our own first-aid kits to remind us of God's love and care for us when we are sick. When God's people were sick, they asked God for help.

Ask What can we do when we don't feel well? Accept suggestions, such as go to the doctor, take medicine, and rest. Remind children that God gives us medicine and doctors to help us.

Say When we are sick or hurt, we can also tell God how we feel and ask Him to make us well! He loves us and will answer our prayer in a way that is best. Have children put the praying hands sticker on an index card or piece of paper and put it inside their first-aid kit.

Ask What else can we do? Show children the sticker of the Bible.

Say We can remember God's promises. He loves us and will take care of us. The best way God showed His love for us was by sending Jesus to take away our sin sickness on the cross. Through Jesus, we have eternal life. That means someday we'll live with Jesus always in heaven where there won't be anymore sickness or hurts or tears.

Give each child the Bible sticker and a card. Have them put the sticker on the

Growing in CHRIST.

card and then place the card into the first-aid kit. Help children turn their first-aid kits over. Point to and read the words "Who saves us?" Jesus! Have the children color the cross or glue yarn or tissue paper to it. Give them a sticker of Jesus to put on this side. They may draw themselves next to Jesus.

Paper Plus option: Provide different colors of chenille wires and pencils. Let the children use their imagination to twist chenille wires together to make a snake. Help them glue wiggle eyes to the snake. (If you use a glue gun, use a low temperature gun and keep it out of reach of the children.) Then help them twist the chenille wire snake around the pencil to make a snake on a pole.

Tell the children that when they use their pencils, they can remember that God saved His people who were bitten by snakes. God saves us through Jesus, who died on the cross to pay for our sins.

When you are done making your snakes, play Pole Tag, a variation of Freeze Tag. Tell one child to pretend to be the snake (It). When the snake tags others, the children become "sick" and must freeze. Children may be unfrozen or "healed" when a "free" child holds up a snake on a pole.

Snack Time

What you do: Provide each child with a pretzel rod and a gummy worm. Let the children wrap the gummy-worm snake on the pretzel pole.

Live It Out

Use your tablet device or smartphone to take a video of the children acting out the story or, if you made them, holding their pencil snakes and telling about the story. Send the video home this week. Encourage children to practice saying "I'm sorry" and "I forgive you" at home.

4 Closing (5 minutes)

Going Home

What you do: Make copies of Activity Page 13B to send home with other take-home items so the children can make their own snakes. Show them how to make the sign of the cross. Tell them this sign reminds them that Jesus saves save them from sin, death, and the devil and gives them eternal life.

Sing "O Sing to the Lord" (*LSB* 808; CD 2) or "Jesus, You Help" (*LOSP*, p. 34)

Say **At the end of church, Pastor often makes a big cross and gives us a blessing from God. The sign of the cross is a reminder that we belong to Jesus and are forgiven. Let's make the sign of the cross and say, "Jesus saves me from my sins. He gives me eternal life."** Do so.

Pray **Dear God, thank You for loving me and taking care of me. You heal me when I'm sick. You take away my sins. Help me always to be thankful. Amen.**

Reflection

Are there any children in your class who appear to have special needs? Have a discussion with the child's parents and ask what you can do to accommodate the child's learning needs.

Sometimes I get sick. What will help me?

Songs and Wiggles-Out Rhymes

Young children must use their large muscles and move around in order to process and learn new information. Incorporate music and movement between periods of quieter learning to allow for this. Give children scarves or ribbon twirlers to use as they sing.

Songs

Cleanup Song
Tune: "Row, Row, Row Your Boat"

Clean, clean, clean the room.
Put our things away.
Help, help, help, help—
Then we'll sing and pray.

Gathering Song
Tune: "Mary Had a Little Lamb"

Come and listen to God's Word,
To God's Word, to God's Word.
Come and listen to God's Word
From His book, the Bible.

Welcome Song
Tune: "The Farmer in the Dell"

Jesus knows my name.
Jesus knows my name.
Jesus knows my name is [Jasper].
Jesus knows my name.

Birthday Song
Tune: "London Bridge Is Falling Down"

We're so glad that you were born,
You were born, you were born.
We're so glad that you were born;
Thank You, Jesus!

Birthday Song
Tune: "Mary Had a Little Lamb"

God chose [child's name] to be His child,
Be His child, be His child.
God chose [child's name] to be His child
Through Baptism and His Word.

Baptism Song
Tune: "London Bridge Is Falling Down"

Thank You, God, for food and drink,
Food and drink, food and drink.
Thank You, God, for food and drink.
How You love us!

Wiggles-Out Rhymes

Wiggles Out

Left foot, right foot, left foot, right foot. *Step in place.*
Make your hands go clap. *Clap once.*
Left foot, right foot, left foot, right foot. *Step in place.*
Make your fingers snap. *Snap once.*
Left foot, right foot, left foot, right foot. *Step in place.*
Turn around real slow. *Turn.*
Left foot, right foot, left foot, right foot. *Step in place.*
In your chair you go. *Sit down.*

Ten Little Fingers

Ten little fingers ready to play. *Wiggle fingers.*
Ten little fingers ready to pray. *Fold hands.*
Help me, dear Jesus, in every way *Bow head.*
To love and serve You every day. *Extend hands.*

God Gave Me

God gave me arms to raise up high. *Raise arms.*
And ten fingers—see them fly. *Wiggle fingers.*
God gave me legs to run, run, run. *Run in place.*
He gave me friends to have some fun. *Point to friend.*
God loves me very much indeed. *Touch heart.*
He gives me everything I need. *Hold hands palms up.*

Clap My Hands

Clap my hands; shout, "Hooray!" *Clap hands.*
Jesus takes my sins away. *Make sign of cross.*
When things go wrong, I stop and pray.
      Fold hands in prayer.
"God, I need Your love today."
      Fold hands over chest for "love."
God loves me. God loves you.
      Point to self; point to classmates.
God helps me forgive you too.
      Point to self; make a cross in the air; point to others.
Clap your hands. Smile and say, *Clap hands.*
"God forgives me!" Shout, "Hooray!"
      Make sign of cross.

From *Fingers Tell the Story*, p. 23,

Supply List

Every Week

Have a Bible, catechism, hymnal, children's songbook, offering basket, puppet, and CD player for use every week, as well as classroom supplies such as scissors, tape, glue, construction paper, stapler, hole punch, yarn or ribbon, and crayons or markers.

Other Supplies

Many of these supplies are for Welcome Time or optional crafts. See each lesson to choose what you want to do; then highlight the supplies you'll need. Paper Plus supplies are listed within the lesson.

Lesson 1

- ❏ Play dough
- ❏ Wiggle eyes, pipe cleaners & other embellishments
- ❏ Decorating supplies
- ❏ Story bag & crumpled drawing
- ❏ CD or paper plates & beanbag
- ❏ Crackers & cans of cheese

Lesson 2

- ❏ Play dough
- ❏ Cookie cutters
- ❏ Crumpled artwork
- ❏ Apple slices

Lesson 3

- ❏ Play dough & toy dishes
- ❏ Story bag
- ❏ Bottle of water, fruit & paper heart
- ❏ Beanbag
- ❏ Bread & toaster
- ❏ Heart & cross cookie cutters
- ❏ Cream cheese or jam

Optional
- ❏ Ring, necklace & robe

Lesson 4

- ❏ Newsprint & cross supplies
- ❏ Straws & embellishments
- ❏ Heart sugar cookies & tubes of frosting or Jell-O jigglers

Optional
- ❏ *Joseph: Jacob's Favorite Son* Arch Book

Lesson 5

- ❏ Tub of rice, towel & hidden objects or dolls & baby-care items
- ❏ Baskets
- ❏ Celery & toppings

Optional
- ❏ Pan of water, play dough & craft sticks; paper cups; green chenille stems (pipe cleaners) or yarn
- ❏ Raffia or twine & fabric
- ❏ *Tiny Baby Moses* Arch Book

Lesson 6

- ❏ Cotton balls
- ❏ Bibles & Bible story books
- ❏ Cell or toy phone
- ❏ Large piece of construction paper
- ❏ Story bag
- ❏ Candle, lighter & shell
- ❏ Picture of a snake
- ❏ Stick pretzels & fruit roll-ups

Optional
- ❏ Yarn

Lesson 7

- ❏ Blocks, toy people & rescue vehicles
- ❏ Story bag
- ❏ Action figures or superhero pictures
- ❏ Cross
- ❏ Rod pretzels or trail mix
- ❏ Plastic zipper bags

Optional
- ❏ *The Ten Plagues* Arch Book
- ❏ Picture of pyramids
- ❏ Black paper
- ❏ Towel & gold bracelets

Lesson 8

- ❏ Paper plates
- ❏ Seasonal decorations
- ❏ Paper plate, yarn & straw or ruler
- ❏ Lamb or cross sugar cookies or pita bread & toppings

Optional
- ❏ Robe, sandals & headpiece

Lesson 9

- ❏ Tub of water
- ❏ Floating objects & toy people
- ❏ Scarves or rhythm instruments
- ❏ Yarn & art supplies
- ❏ Blue gelatin & jelly beans

Optional
- ❏ Storybooks or pictures of fears
- ❏ *Moses' Dry Feet* Arch Book

Lesson 10

- ❏ Paper plates
- ❏ Grocery sack & groceries
- ❏ Beanbag
- ❏ Nilla wafers & water

Optional
- ❏ Magazine pictures or play dough
- ❏ *Moses and the Long Walk* Arch Book

Lesson 11

- ❏ Picture of Jesus or a cross
- ❏ Gift bags
- ❏ Traditional twist pretzels

Optional
- ❏ Colored paper or play dough
- ❏ *The Ten Commandments* Arch Book

Lesson 12

- ❏ Church props (hymnals, offering plate, bowl for font, doll)
- ❏ Pictures of church items
- ❏ Decorating supplies for craft banner
- ❏ Graham crackers & frosting or cheese

Optional
- ❏ Blocks, towel, paper cups

Lesson 13

- ❏ Toy medical kit
- ❏ Bandages & dolls
- ❏ Paper bag or gift bag
- ❏ Medical props (bandage, lip balm, tissues, heating pad)
- ❏ Pencil or ruler
- ❏ Index cards
- ❏ Pretzels & gummy worms

Optional
- ❏ Play dough
- ❏ *Moses and the Bronze Snake* Arch Book